Encountering God's Missionary Spirit

A Missional Study of the Holy Spirit

Mark R. Turney

AIA Publications
Springfield, MO USA

Encountering God's Missionary Spirit: A Missional Study of the Holy Spirit. Copyright © 2018 Mark R. Turney. All rights reserved. No portion of this book may be reproduced, stored in a retrieval system, or transmitted in any form or by any means—electronic, mechanical, photocopy, recording, or any other—except for brief quotations in printed reviews, without the prior written permission of the publisher.

Unless otherwise specified, Scripture quotations used in this book are taken from the 2011 edition of the Holy Bible, New International Version®. NIV®. Copyright © 1973, 1978, 1984, 2011 by Biblica, Inc. ™ Used by permission of Zondervan. All rights reserved worldwide.www.zondervan.com. The "NIV" and "New International Version" are trademarks registered in the United States Patent and Trademark Office by Biblica, Inc™

Scriptures references marked NASB are taken from the NEW AMERICAN STANDARD BIBLE®, copyright© 1960, 1962, 1963, 1968, 1971, 1972, 1973, 1975, 1977, 1995 by The Lockman Foundation. Used by permission.

Turney, Mark R., 1968—
Encountering God's Missionary Spirit: A Missional Study of the Holy Spirit / Mark R. Turney

1. Bible 2. Theology 3. Pentecostal 4. Pneumatology 5. Holy Spirit 6. Missions

ISBN: 978-0-9997032-0-5

Printed in the United States of America
AIA Publications
Springfield, MO USA 65802
www.ActsInAfrica.org
www.DecadeOfPentecost.org

To my wife Victoria;
my love, best friend, and collaborer in missions.
Your love, encouragement, and suggestions
made this book possible. I could not
have done it without you.

To Denny Miller,
mentor and dearly beloved friend.
So much of what is contained in this book
the Lord taught me through you.
Your guidance and suggestions influenced
every part. It is as much a fruit
of your labor as mine.

Contents

Introduction 1

Part One ~ The Holy Spirit: The Spirit of Missions 3

    1. Introduction to Pneumatology 5

    2. The Holy Spirit A Divine Person 21

    3. The Holy Spirit: A Missionary Spirit 39

Part Two ~ The Missionary Spirit in the Old Testament 59

    4. The Missionary Spirit Prepares God's People 61

    5. The Missionary Spirit Reveals God's Mission 81

Part Three ~ The Missionary Spirit in the New Testament 99

    6. The Missionary Spirit in Jesus 101

    7. The Missionary Spirit In The Church 123

    8. The Missionary Spirit In Personal Experience 143

Part Four ~ Empowered by the Missionary Spirit 167

    9. Baptism in the Holy Spirit: Its Missional Purpose 169

    10. Baptism in the Holy Spirit: Its Missional Signs 193

    11. Ministry in the Spirit 217

Bibliography 241

Introduction

This is a book on pneumatology, the branch of Christian theology concerned with the person and work of the Holy Spirit. The book, however, approaches the study of the Holy Spirit from a unique biblical perspective. It is a *missional* pneumatology. It focuses on the central role of the Holy Spirit in fulfilling the *missio Dei,* or the mission of God. God's mission is to call to himself a people out of every tribe, language, and nation on earth. This book presents the Holy Spirit as "God's Missionary Spirit."

Unfortunately, much teaching on the Holy Spirit today largely ignores the Holy Spirit's role in God's mission. It focuses rather, almost exclusively, on the Spirit's work in individual Christians to enrich their lives personally. While this emphasis is valid, when divorced from the Spirit's primary work of enabling God's people to fulfill God's mission, it becomes a self-centered distortion of truth. Today, during these last days of time, God's people must regain a biblical, missional understanding of the person and work of the Holy Spirit. The church can only function as Christ intended when believers are empowered by God's Spirit and committed to carrying out God's mission in the earth. This is the central thesis of this study.

This book is written primarily for Pentecostal pastors and church leaders in Africa. It is intended to equip them to better lead their churches into authentic Pentecostal experience and practice. It is further designed to help church leaders mobilize their churches for Spirit-empowered mission and church planting. The book can also serve as a valuable resource for anyone who wants to better understand the person and work of the Holy Spirit, and who longs to experience His powerful working their life.

Introduction

As you study the lessons in this book, you will learn how the Spirit of God stands ready to empower you and enable you to participate effectively in God's mission. In doing this, you will discover the essential role of an experience known as the baptism in the Holy Spirit in transforming believers into powerful witnesses for Christ. You will also learn from biblical directives and examples how you can effectively minister in the power of the Holy Spirit as did Jesus and His first disciples.

The church can fulfill its God ordained purpose only when it is empowered by the Holy Spirit, allowing it to faithfully march in step with God's Missionary Spirit as He moves to carry out God's mission on earth. If the church of Africa is to fulfill its God-ordained destiny among the nations, it must recapture a biblical, missional understanding of the person and work of the Holy Spirit. It must fully embrace Jesus' last message to the church:

> *But you will receive power*
> *when the Holy Spirit comes on you;*
> *and you will be my witnesses in Jerusalem,*
> *and in all Judea and Samaria,*
> *and to the ends of the earth.*
> (Acts 1:8)

~ Part One ~

The Holy Spirit: The Spirit of Missions

~ CHAPTER 1 ~

Introduction to Pneumatology

You are beginning the exciting and important study known as *pneumatology*. The word *pneumatology* comes from ancient Greek. *Pneuma* means spirit and *logy* means study, knowledge, or doctrine. Thus, Pneumatology is the study of what the Bible teaches about the person and work of the Holy Spirit.

WHY STUDY PNEUMATOLOGY?

Throughout this study you will discover many reasons why it is essential for you to understand the work of the Holy Spirit and to experience His power and presence in your life and ministry. Perhaps the most important reason is that the Holy Spirit is at work empowering and leading the church to complete the Father's mission to save the nations through the proclamation of the gospel of Jesus Christ. This book will help you prepare to join in that mission. It will help you learn how to teach others about the Holy Spirit and lead them to experience His power and presence so they, too, may be empowered as witnesses for Christ. Throughout this study, we will repeatedly highlight a theme of the relationship between the work of the Holy Spirit and the mission of God.

As you study what the Bible teaches about the Holy Spirit, you will discover who He is, what He is like, and how He works in the lives of people. While it is foundational for us to know what the Bible says about the Holy Spirit, we must not stop there. If we are truly to be Pentecostal Christians, we must experience His powerful work in our own lives. This is possible if we spend time in earnest prayer, seeking to be filled with, and remaining full of, the Holy Spirit.

Several years ago, I was in a meeting with African leaders from several countries. The speaker was teaching on the work of the Holy Spirit. He made a simple declaration that grabbed my attention. He said, "We learn about the Holy Spirit from the Scriptures. However, there is only one way to experience Him. We experience Him as we seek Him in prayer." God used that statement to awaken in me a renewed desire to seek the power and presence of the Holy Spirit. I encourage you as well to dedicate time in prayer each day to ask God to fill you with His Spirit. Invite the Holy Spirit to fill you with His presence and to be your teacher and guide as you seek to learn about Him from the Scriptures He inspired.

Consequences of Neglecting Pneumatology

The church today must not neglect to emphasize the person and work of the Holy Spirit as it relates to the mission of God. History shows that neglecting the Holy Spirit results in negative consequences for the mission of God and the life of the church.

The Holy Spirit worked powerfully in the early church. In time, however, the church stopped emphasizing the Holy Spirit in its teaching and preaching. During the eighth and ninth centuries, the church was almost entirely driven out of the Middle East and North Africa by the growth of Islam. Europe then became the center of the church's influence. Beginning in the period known as the Renaissance, western civilization began to emphasize rational thinking and the scientific method. As a result, westerners, including those in the church, began to reject the idea of the supernatural. Consequently, the church relegated the dynamic work of the Spirit, as described in the book of Acts, to an era no longer considered relevant for today. The years of neglect caused the church to decline spiritually and to lose its dynamic power to accomplish God's mission of proclaiming the gospel to all nations.

In the early 1900s God began to pour out His Spirit again, resulting in the modern Pentecostal revival. This outpouring came through a renewed emphasis on the Bible's teaching regarding the Holy Spirit. As the church once again began to study the Scriptures concerning the Holy Spirit, a renewed desire awoke in many peoples hearts to experience the Holy Spirit like the early Christians in the book of Acts. God answered their prayers by pouring out His Spirit. Because of this renewed emphasis on the Holy Spirit, during the twentieth century the Pentecostal church became the fastest growing segment of the church worldwide.

Throughout this study we will examine scriptural truths that support a repeated pattern in church history. The church thrives and grows when it emphasizes the work and power of the Holy Spirit to fulfill God's mission to proclaim Christ to the nations. However, when the church loses this missional focus, it begins to falter. If the church is to continue to move forward, it must maintain and nurture the Pentecostal revival that began in the twentieth century. May what Paul said of the church in Galatia not be said of the church today: "Are you so foolish? After beginning by means of the Spirit, are you now trying to finish by means of the flesh?" (Galatians 3:3).

Chapter 1 ~ Introduction to Pneumatology

HISTORICAL AND MODERN ERRORS

This study is important because in Africa today, many people misunderstand the Holy Spirit and some hold harmful ideas about Him and His work. If the church is going to experience a genuine work of the Spirit and participate in the mission of God, it must walk in the truth of God's Word (John 4:23–24).

Early Errors

During its early centuries, the church faced several challenges concerning the doctrine of the Holy Spirit. In the second century, some men like Origen and Justin Martyr proposed that the Father, Son, and Spirit were not all equal as God. According to their teaching, the Father was superior to Jesus the Son, who was also superior to the Holy Spirit. Teachings like this opened the door for a diminishing respect and emphasis on the person and work of the Holy Spirit.

Another serious theological challenge is known as *Sabellianism*. In the third century A.D., a church leader named Sabellius rejected the doctrine of the Trinity, which correctly describes God as being one God who is manifested in three distinct Persons. Instead, he emphasized the absolute unity of God, and taught that God is one God who revealed, or manifested, himself in three "modes" or aspects in different historical eras. Sabellius argued that in the Old Testament, God revealed himself in the mode of the Father; in the Gospels, God revealed himself as the Son; and in the age of the church, He revealed himself as the Holy Spirit. In other words, Sabellius taught that God is not three distinct Persons, but rather one Person with three different names and roles. The early church rejected Sabellius' teaching and condemned it as heretical.

Modern Errors

In recent history, a modern form of Sabellianism has been revived. One segment of the Pentecostal movement known as

Oneness Pentecostalism holds to a similar teaching. Like Sabellius, they reject the doctrine of the Trinity and teach that God is only one Person who manifests himself in different modes or roles. Oneness Pentecostal churches are sometimes known as "Jesus Only" churches because of their insistence that water baptism must be administered in Jesus' name rather than in the name of the Father, Son, and Holy Spirit. They also normally equate the baptism in the Holy Spirit, accompanied by the evidence of speaking in tongues, with salvation. Such a teaching lessens the missional impact of Spirit baptism on a believer's life because it downplays the empowering work of the Spirit in favor of His work of regeneration (Acts 1:8; 2:38–39).

Another modern error is the idea that the Holy Spirit is an impersonal force or energy like electricity. For example, the Jehovah's Witnesses deny the doctrine of the Trinity and argue that the Holy Spirit is simply the "active force" of God. They deny that the Bible presents the Holy Spirit as a distinct Person, and they use lower-case letters for names and titles like "holy spirit." The Jehovah's Witnesses have even changed many passages in their New World Translation of the Bible to support these erroneous teachings.

A further danger related to the error that the Holy Spirit is a force or energy is the idea that His power can be controlled or used in any way that people wish. Even some who call themselves Pentecostals treat the Holy Spirit as if He were a magical power rather than the third Person of the Trinity. The Holy Spirit, however, is not a force to be controlled by our will or desire. This study will show that He is God and therefore requires our submission and obedience. Across Africa, people participate in many practices designed to gain and control spiritual power. We must be careful to never allow unbiblical concepts related to the manipulation of spiritual power to guide our understanding of the work of the Holy Spirit. That is an important reason for this biblical study on pneumatology.

Chapter 1 ~ Introduction to Pneumatology

HOW NON-PENTECOSTALS AND PENTECOSTALS APPROACH PNEUMATOLOGY

As we begin this study of pneumatology, we need to establish a few foundational principles to use in examining, interpreting, and applying what the Bible says concerning the work of the Holy Spirit. Not all theologians agree about the guidelines for this task. Therefore, in this section and the next we will examine some significant differences between how Pentecostals and non-Pentecostals deal with the study of pneumatology and the book of Acts.[1]

Characteristics of a Non-Pentecostal Approach

Priority Given to Pauline Pneumatology over Lukan Pneumatology

In Part 3, we will examine three overarching categories in which the New Testament presents the work of the Holy Spirit in regard to personal experience. These are salvation, sanctification, and empowerment for service. All three need a proper emphasis for a balanced biblical understanding of the work of the Holy Spirit. Many non-Pentecostals, however, primarily emphasize the work of the Spirit in salvation and sanctification and largely ignore the aspect of empowerment for service. This results from a pattern of elevating Paul's pneumatology over Luke's. Paul's epistles focus more on the work of the Holy Spirit in salvation and sanctification, with a few references to the empowering work of the Spirit. Luke's Gospel and

---

[1] The terms "Pentecostal" and "Non-Pentecostal" are broad terms that include many branches of Christian churches. In this book Pentecostal refers to Classical Pentecostals who trace their origin and doctrine to the Azusa Street revival at the beginning of the twentieth century. Non-Pentecostal refers to Evangelicals and Protestants who believe the Bible is the inspired Word of God, but they interpret Spirit baptism as the new birth (1 Cor. 12:13), rather than a separate experience that empowers believers for witness, as Classical Pentecostals believe (Acts 1:8).

Acts focus almost exclusively on the work of the Holy Spirit to empower believers for service. Focusing primarily on Paul's presentation of the Holy Spirit, while largely ignoring Luke's, results in an unbalanced understanding of the work of the Spirit.[2]

Baptism in the Holy Spirit Equals Salvation

Non-Pentecostals typically do not believe that the baptism in the Holy Spirit is an empowering experience subsequent to and distinct from salvation. Rather, many non-Pentecostals argue that the baptism in the Holy Spirit and salvation are the same thing. They also argue that the signs accompanying Pentecost, including speaking in tongues, were not intended to be repeated. They teach that Pentecost marks the beginning of the new covenant God has made through Christ. As a result, they view Pentecost as the "birthday of the church."

Charismatic Work of the Spirit Has Ceased

Many non-Pentecostals believe that the supernatural working of the Spirit ceased when the early apostles died. As a result, they reject the idea that the Spirit of God still works today through healing the sick and casting out demon spirits. They argue that the supernatural manifestations of the Spirit, which were so prominent in the New Testament church, have ceased to function. This includes gifts such as speaking in tongues, prophecy, a message of wisdom, and other supernatural manifestations of the Spirit mentioned in the New Testament (Acts 2:4; 1 Corinthians 12:8–10). Because of this claim,

---

[2] The following books are good sources for further study of this issue. Roger Stronstad. *The Charismatic Theology of St. Luke.* (Peabody, MA: Hendrickson, 1984)., Denzil R. Miller. *Empowered for Global Mission: A Missionary Look at the Book of Acts.* (Springfield, MO: Life Publishers, 2005)., William W. and Robert P. Menzies. *Spirit and Power: Foundations of Pentecostal Experience.* (Grand Rapids, MI: Zondervan, 2000).

these non-Pentecostals are sometimes known as "cessationists." Some have suggested that the charismatic working of the Spirit was reserved for a special dispensation of the Spirit that only lasted during the founding years of the church. Non-Pentecostal Christians generally believe that the Holy Spirit is at work in the world today; however, they contend that the Spirit works primarily through the Word of God to save and sanctify people.

Characteristics of a Pentecostal Approach

Every Biblical Author's Pneumatology Is Equally Valued

The Pentecostal approach to pneumatology is guided by certain foundational principles of interpreting and applying Scriptures related to the Holy Spirit. To begin with, Pentecostal scholars believe that each biblical author's presentation of the Holy Spirit should be valued equally. The fact that non-Pentecostals often give priority to Paul's epistles over Luke and Acts implies that they view some parts of Scripture as being more authoritative than others. However, Pentecostals affirm that each biblical author's presentation of the Holy Spirit is equally inspired by God and should be equally valued (2 Timothy 3:16).

The three New Testament authors who wrote the most concerning the Holy Spirit are Luke, Paul, and John. Each one should be allowed to speak out of his own context and purpose in writing. Moreover, each should be allowed to contribute to our understanding of the person and work of the Holy Spirit. Further, while the Old Testament authors admittedly deal less with the work of the Holy Spirit than those of the New Testament, they also present important aspects of the work of the Spirit that contribute to a richer pneumatology. Pentecostals recognize that each of these authors wrote a unique message concerning the work of the Holy Spirit, and it is a message that needs to be communicated to God's people. A Pentecostal approach allows each author to make his own contribution and then combines their teachings into a fuller, more balanced pneumatology—one that recognizes all the working of the Spirit seen in Scripture. This approach will guide us through our study of pneumatology.

Baptism in the Holy Spirit Is Distinct from Salvation

Pentecostals believe that Christ promised a baptism in the Holy Spirit as a work of the Spirit separate from salvation (Acts 1:4–5). The purpose of this experience is to empower believers for witness and service to Christ and His mission of proclaiming the gospel to the "ends of the earth" (Acts 1:8). Belief in this experience was the primary starting point of the Pentecostal revival in the early 1900s, which brought about the formation of the modern Pentecostal church. The experience of Spirit baptism is so foundational to Pentecostal pneumatology that an entire section of this study is dedicated to examining the experience and its implications for the church.

Supernatural Work of the Spirit Continues Today

Pentecostals also believe that the supernatural work of the Spirit was not reserved for one special dispensation at the founding of the church. Rather, they approach the study of pneumatology with the firm conviction that all the charismatic gifts of the Spirit that operated in the New Testament church are equally available and necessary for the church today. This belief in the current supernatural work of the Spirit will bring focus to our presentation of the Holy Spirit in this study. It will help us connect what the Holy Spirit did in the Bible and what He does today.

Emphasis on Empowerment for Mission

A Pentecostal approach to the study of pneumatology holds that the Holy Spirit is intricately and essentially involved in the fulfillment of God's mission to redeem people "from every tribe and language and people and nation" (Revelation 5:9). For Pentecostals, the study of pneumatology is not just a matter of correct theology; it is an essential element to the church's fulfillment of the Great Commission (Luke 24:46–49). Pentecostals believe that the power of the Holy Spirit is necessary for effective witness and proclamation of the gospel (Luke 4:18–19; Acts 1:8). Therefore, we will approach pneumatology with an intent to discover how the Holy Spirit can enable the church to fulfill the mission of God.

HOW NON-PENTECOSTALS AND PENTECOSTALS APPROACH THE BOOK OF ACTS

The book of Acts is at the heart of the differences between a Pentecostal and a non-Pentecostal approach to pneumatology. Pentecostals read the book of Acts differently than non-Pentecostals. This understanding is essential to the unique Pentecostal approach to pneumatology.

Characteristics of a Non-Pentecostal Approach

Normative Doctrine and Practice Not Found in the Book of Acts

The Bible consists of many different genres, or types, of literature, such as poetry, prophecy, parables, laws, letters, and historical narrative. Sound hermeneutics requires that interpreters take into account these different types of literature. Unfortunately, many theologians argue that narrative portions of Scripture, such as Luke and Acts, have little or no value for establishing normative doctrine and practice as a standard for all believers. They contend that narrative merely describes what has happened, so it is not didactic and thus intended to teach doctrine. Instead, they declare that one must go to the direct teachings of Jesus and the apostles to find normative doctrine. They conclude that since the book of Acts is narrative literature, it serves only to describe what took place in the early church—or possibly to illustrate what is clearly taught in other so-called didactic portions of Scripture. Based on this principle, they

accuse Pentecostals of wrongly using Acts as a basis for establishing normative doctrine and practice.

Luke's Purpose Was Primarily Historical

An important hermeneutical principle that affects the way one reads the book of Acts is *authorial intent*. This principle contends that God's word to us today is found within the purpose and intended meaning of the original author.[3] A balanced perspective on authorial intent recognizes that the intended meaning of the human author flows from what was intended and inspired by the Holy Spirit.

The vital question then is what was Luke's intention in writing the book of Acts? The answer to that question will determine how you read and interpret Acts. Many non-Pentecostals argue that Luke's intention in writing Acts was merely to record history. In other words, his purpose was simply to describe how the church began and rapidly grew from its small beginnings in Jerusalem to the then-known "ends of the earth." Based on this conclusion, non-Pentecostals argue that it is wrong to claim that the example of the early church in the book of Acts should serve as a pattern for the church today. Their belief that Luke's intention was primarily historical wrongfully closes the door to drawing any connection between what happened in the church in Acts and what should happen in the church today.

---

[3] The belief that Scripture was inspired by the Holy Spirit is included. Therefore the intended meaning of the human author flows from what was intended and inspired by the divine author – the Holy Spirit.

Characteristics of a Pentecostal Approach

Biblical Narrative Is Didactic in Purpose

As was stated earlier, Pentecostals read the book of Acts differently than non-Pentecostals. They believe that Luke wrote the book of Acts not only to describe what happened in the early church but also to teach believers through the model of the Spirit's work in the early church. A Pentecostal approach to pneumatology stands on the assumption that biblical narrative, including the book of Acts, was written with a didactic purpose.

In support of this belief, Pentecostal theologian Roger Stronstad argues that the separation between history and teaching is not found in the New Testament. He points out how Paul taught in his epistles that "all Scripture is God-breathed and is useful for teaching [or doctrine]" (2 Timothy 3:16) and that "everything that was written in the past was written to teach us" (Romans 15:4), including the narrative portions of the Old Testament. Stronstad reasons that if Paul believed that the Old Testament had lessons to teach Christians, then it only makes sense that Luke, who modeled his history of the early church after Old Testament history, also wrote to teach universal truth.[4]

Most Africans understand this truth. They naturally understand that stories of past events can teach great lessons for life. Much of the wisdom and knowledge found in traditional African societies is taught with stories. The concept that the narrative portions of Scripture are only descriptive, having no didactic value, is an unscriptural, Western perspective. It is a perspective that Pentecostals reject.

Luke's Purpose Was Theological and Missional

A Pentecostal approach to interpreting Acts presupposes that

---

[4] Roger Stronstad, *The Charismatic Theology of St. Luke* (Peabody, MA: Hendrickson, 1984), 6–7.

Luke chose to use historical narrative to convey the message that he wanted the church to hear. His intent, however, was more than just retelling history. He wanted the church to understand that the power of the Holy Spirit (theological intent) is the key to fulfilling Christ's command to proclaim the gospel to all nations (missional intent). We understand this from Jesus' own words cited by Luke in Acts 1:8: "But you will receive power when the Holy Spirit comes on you; and you will be my witnesses in Jerusalem, and in all Judea and Samaria, and to the ends of the earth." These final words of Jesus serve as the "interpretive key" to the entire book of Acts.[5]

Acts Establishes a Normative Pattern for the Church of All Ages

The fact that Luke wrote Acts with clear didactic and missional intent leads us to the conclusion that the book of Acts contains a normative pattern for the church until Jesus comes again. Pentecostal theologians unashamedly affirm this powerful truth. In the following chapters, we will examine those normative doctrines and practices in more detail.

A word of caution is appropriate at this point. While we as Pentecostals affirm that normative doctrine and practice can indeed be found in the book of Acts, we contend that such doctrine and practice must not contradict what is clearly taught in other portions of Scripture. This balancing principle will help keep us within the bounds of sound biblical doctrine.

IMPLICATIONS AND APPLICATIONS

At the end of each chapter in this study, we will ask, "What are some implications and applications of the truths that we have examined?" Of course, there are many more possibilities than those

---

[5] Denzil R. Miller, *Empowered for Global Mission: A Missionary Look at the Book of Acts* (Springfield, MO: Life Publishers International, 2005), 83.

included here. As you prayerfully reflect on the Scriptures and the truths you are studying, the Holy Spirit will give you further insight into how to apply what you are learning to your own life and ministry context.

Our Experience of the Holy Spirit

In this lesson, we discussed the need to not only learn *about* the Holy Spirit and His work but to *experience* His presence and powerful work. We also noted how neglect and misunderstandings concerning the nature and work of the Holy Spirit have hindered His work in fulfilling the mission of God. This implies that all believers have a personal responsibility to understand and experience the powerful working of the Spirit in their own life and that all believers must fully commit themselves to God and His mission to redeem the nations.

We also discussed the Pentecostal belief that the Spirit is involved both in our salvation and in a second and vital experience called the baptism in the Holy Spirit. This implies that if we are to experience the full work of the Spirit in our lives, we must intentionally emphasize and seek this experience. If you have never experienced the baptism in the Holy Spirit as described in the book of Acts, the most important application of this lesson in your personal life would be to ask God to give you this experience.

How We Study and Teach the Scriptures

The fact that there are many different opinions and perspectives on the Holy Spirit is sobering. This demonstrates a great need for us to clearly and scripturally define our beliefs concerning the Holy Spirit. In doing this, we must humbly ask Him to help us.

The many misunderstandings concerning the Spirit also make us aware of the need to teach frequently in the church about the person and work of the Spirit. Every Christian must understand who the

Spirit is and how He can prepare them for life and service to God. If we fail in this responsibility, most believers will remain uninformed about the power of the Spirit to work in their lives. Without leaders who teach about the Holy Spirit and lead the church into seeking Him, the church could easily become a lifeless institution that makes no eternal difference in the world.

Our Participation in the Mission of God

We have learned that the church has received a commission from Christ to proclaim the gospel to all people. However, many Christians and churches have been unsuccessful in fulfilling their role in that mission. Their level of effectiveness ultimately depends on their level of empowerment by the Holy Spirit. Above all else, this truth should motivate us to diligently seek to experience the Spirit on an ongoing basis. The salvation of our neighbors and the nations depends on a church empowered by the Spirit as we see in the book of Acts.

Questions for Discussion and Reflection

1. Do you see any neglect of pneumatology in the church today, and if so what result or consequences have you observed?
2. What errors concerning the person and work of the Holy Spirit are affecting the church or churches you work with?
3. What can you do to counteract neglect or errors in the church concerning the Holy Spirit?
4. Compare how a Pentecostal approach to pneumatology might affect ministry and missions in the church as opposed to a non-Pentecostal approach to pneumatology.
5. Compare how a Pentecostal approach to the book of Acts might affect your teaching and preaching as opposed to a non-Pentecostal approach to the book of Acts.

~ CHAPTER 2 ~

The Holy Spirit
A Divine Person

Some people think they can manipulate the Holy Spirit similar to the way a witchdoctor manipulates spiritual power. They see the Holy Spirit as a spiritual force or energy to use for their own purposes. It is true that the Holy Spirit is powerful, but He is more than just power. The Spirit is a divine Person. He is present and working in the world to accomplish the mission of God.

In this chapter we will begin to discover who the Holy Spirit really is. He is the missionary Spirit of God! By discussing His personhood, His attributes, His names, and His symbols, we will learn more about His character and work. All along, we will apply what we have learned to our own lives and ministries as we participate in God's mission.

THE HOLY SPIRIT IS A PERSON

The Bible affirms that the Holy Spirit is a Person. Because of this, we can know, love, and obey Him. Since He is the missionary Spirit of God, we can also work together with Him to accomplish God's mission.

Sometimes people think that because He is called the Spirit, He is merely a force of some kind. As a result, they wrongly refer to the Holy Spirit as "it." However, personhood does not require that one have a physical body. God the Father does not have a physical body, and before His incarnation, the Son did not have a physical body (Hebrews 10:5). Yet they have always existed as Persons. Likewise, the Holy Spirit is a Person and possesses all the characteristics of personhood.

His Personhood Is Seen in His Works

The works of the Holy Spirit demonstrate His personhood. The Bible describes how the Holy Spirit does things that only a person can do. For example:

- He creates (Job 33:4; Psalm 104:30).
- He convicts sinners to turn them to God (Genesis 6:3; John 16:8).
- He speaks (John 16:13; Acts 8:29; 10:19; Revelation 2:7).
- He teaches (Luke 12:12; John 14:26).
- He testifies (John 15:26; Romans 8:16; 1 Peter 1:11).
- He guides (John 16:13).
- He intercedes (Romans 8:26).
- He comforts (Acts 9:31).
- He forbids (Acts 16:6).
- He works miracles (Acts 8:39; Romans 1:3–4).

These works of the Holy Spirit, and others, show that He is indeed a divine Person.

His Personhood Is Seen in His Characteristics

We also find evidence of the Spirit's personhood in certain personal characteristics that the Bible ascribes to Him. These characteristics are related to the three attributes of personality: the mind, the emotions, and the will.

- He has a *mind,* meaning He thinks and is intelligent (Romans 8:27; 1 Corinthians 2:10–11).
- He can be rebelled against, blasphemed, and lied to, causing Him to grieve, which demonstrates that He has *emotions* (Isaiah 63:10; Luke 12:10; Acts 5:3; Ephesians 4:30).
- He makes choices, which demonstrates that He has a *will* (Acts 13:2; 16:6–7; 1 Corinthians 12:11).

His Personhood Is Seen in the Fellowship We Have with Him

Paul twice mentioned the potential for us to have fellowship with the Spirit (2 Corinthians 13:14; Philippians 2:1). To have fellowship means to enjoy a relationship with someone. This relationship includes friendship and partnership with someone who shares our interests. What a blessing to know that the Holy Spirit is a Person with whom we can have such fellowship. When we are busy working in God's harvest field, we know that the Holy Spirit is there to empower and encourage us in the work (Matthew 28:20; Acts 1:8).

His Personhood Is Seen in His Membership in the Trinity.

Theologians sometimes use the word *Trinity* to describe how God exists as three distinct yet interrelated and unified Persons: Father, Son, and Holy Spirit. While the word *Trinity* does not appear in the Bible, the concept is supported throughout Scripture. The word means "tri-unity" or "three-in-oneness." The doctrine of the Trinity states that the Father, Son, and Spirit are three distinct Persons who are each fully God, yet in essence are one God. They are not three Gods, nor are they three parts of one God. They are one God in three Persons. The Holy Spirit is sometimes referred to as the "third Person in the Trinity." Therefore, just as the Father is a divine Person, and the Son is a divine Person, the Holy Spirit is also a divine Person. Together they are one God.

The concept of the Trinity, like many of the core doctrines of the church, is progressively revealed throughout Scripture. The Old Testament gives glimpses of the Trinity (for example, Genesis 1:26; 3:22; Isaiah 48:16) but emphasizes the fact that God is one (Deuteronomy 6:4). This emphasis on the unity of God was necessary in the polytheistic context in which Israel lived. The nations needed to know that the many gods they served were false gods and that there is only one true God.

The New Testament, however, presents a more fully developed presentation of God. There He is clearly revealed to be three Persons, yet one God. Christians today are privileged to read the Old Testament with deeper understanding concerning the person and work of the Holy Spirit based on the full revelation of Scripture. This understanding enables us to cooperate more effectively with God the Holy Spirit in fulfilling God's mission to redeem the nations.

THE HOLY SPIRIT IS GOD

Chapter 1 mentioned some false ideas that people hold about the Holy Spirit, ideas that deny His deity. However, as mentioned above, the Bible clearly describes the Holy Spirit as being *fully God* along with the Father and the Son. Peter declared to Ananias and Sapphira that when they lied to the Holy Spirit, they had lied to God (Acts 5:3–4). Let us look further at what the Bible says about the deity of the Holy Spirit.

His Deity Is Seen in His Attributes

There are certain attributes (qualities or characteristics) that are uniquely associated with God. The Bible ascribes these attributes to the Holy Spirit just as it does to the Father and the Son. Three of those attributes are omniscience, omnipotence, and omnipresence, as follows:

Omniscience. When we say that God is omniscient, we mean that He knows everything (1 John 3:20). He knows everything that exists (Hebrews 4:13), and He knows everything that has happened in the past and that will happen in the future (Isaiah 42:8–9; 46:9–10). He even knows our thoughts and motives (Psalm 139:1–2; 1 Corinthians 4:5). The Holy Spirit knows these things as well. Paul declared, "The Spirit searches all things, even the deep things of God…no one knows the thoughts of God except the Spirit of God" (1 Corinthians 2:10–11).

Omnipotence. When we say that God is omnipotent, we mean that He has all power and can do anything (Jeremiah 32:17; Mark 10:27). Likewise, the Holy Spirit can do anything. For example, this is demonstrated in the miraculous birth of Christ to the virgin Mary (Luke 1:26–33). The angel Gabriel told Mary that the Holy Spirit would come upon her and cause her to conceive the Christ child. He explained to her that this could happen because "nothing is impossible with God" (1:35, 37). Throughout the Bible, the deity of the Holy Spirit is repeatedly demonstrated through His powerful works.

Omnipresence. When we say that God is omnipresent, we mean that He is present everywhere in creation all the time (Jeremiah 23:23–24). The Holy Spirit is also omnipresent. This further demonstrates that He is God. David declared that there was nowhere in all creation that he could go to get away from the presence of God's Spirit (Psalm 139:7–10).

His Names Reveal Other Divine Attributes

Three of the Spirit's names reveal other attributes that demonstrate His diety:

The Eternal Spirit. God is eternal (Psalm 90:2; Isaiah 40:28). This means He has no beginning and He will have no end. He created all that exists. The Holy Spirit is called the "Eternal Spirit" (Hebrews 9:14), which affirms that He is God.

The Holy Spirit. God is also holy (Psalm 99:9). This means He is pure, without sin, and perfect in every way possible. The name used most often in the Bible for the Spirit of God is the "Holy Spirit." This emphasis on the holiness of the Spirit is another indication that He is God.

The Spirit of God/Christ. The names *Spirit of God* and *Spirit of Christ* also identify the Holy Spirit as being God (Matthew 12:28; Romans 8:9). He is not a created Spirit but is the Spirit of God the Father and God the Son.

His Deity Is Seen in His Relationship with the Father and Son

In several biblical passages, the Holy Spirit is mentioned coequally with the Father and Jesus Christ. These statements indicate that while He is distinct from the Father and Son, He is closely related to them. These passages also imply that the Holy Spirit is God together with the Father and the Son. Here are some examples from Scripture:

- The *Spirit* coming on Jesus, the *Son,* in the form of a dove at His baptism, and the *Father* speaking from heaven (Matthew 3:16–17; Mark 1:9–11; Luke 3:21–23).
- Jesus' command to baptize disciples in the name of the *Father* and of the *Son* and of the *Holy Spirit* (Matthew 28:19).

- Paul's benediction: "May the grace of the *Lord Jesus Christ,* and the love of *God,* and the fellowship of the *Holy Spirit* be with you all" (2 Corinthians 13:14, emphasis added).

NAMES OF THE HOLY SPIRIT

We can learn much about the Holy Spirit by studying His names. When you meet someone for the first time, it is important to learn that person's name so you can correctly identify him or her. Similar to most African cultures, names in the Bible often have deep meaning. They describe important characteristics about a person. The Bible uses various names for the Holy Spirit. While some of the names can be considered titles, they nevertheless function like names and help us know the Spirit better. As we study His names, we will see how they also reveal His work in God's mission.

Holy Spirit

Holy Spirit is the most common name used in the Bible for God's Spirit. The name *Holy Spirit* is used three times in the Old Testament and ninety-three times in the New Testament. In another related verse, He is called the "Spirit of holiness" (Romans 1:4). To be holy is to be morally pure and perfect, without any connection to sin or evil. According to L. Thomas Holdcroft, this name, and its wide usage in Scripture, emphasizes that the Spirit's "special task is to implement the divine holiness within humans and throughout the universe…[and it] serves to distinguish Him from all the unholy spirits that are at work in the world."[6]

God's Word repeatedly declares that we must be holy as God is holy (Leviticus 11:44, 45; 19:2; 20:7, 26; 1 Peter 1:16). God now seeks to redeem fallen humanity and to make us holy and restore us to

---

[6] L. Thomas Holdcroft, *The Holy Spirit: A Pentecostal Interpretation,* Revised. (Abbotsford, Canada: CeeTec Publishing, 1999), 17.

the perfect communion He had with Adam and Eve in the beginning of creation. Only then can we be God's special people and truly represent Him to the nations. We can live holy lives only through faith in the shed blood of Jesus and by the power of the Holy Spirit.

Spirit of God / Spirit of the Lord

The next most commonly used names for the Holy Spirit in Scripture are the related names *Spirit of God* (used twenty-six times) and *Spirit of the Lord* (used twenty-seven times). These names point to the special relationship between the Holy Spirit and God the Father.

In the Old Testament, the Hebrew word *Elohim* is the general word for God who is the Creator of all things. There are many spirits in the world, but only one Spirit of God, the true Creator of the universe.

The name *Yahweh,* which is translated as *Lord* throughout the Old Testament, is the personal, or covenantal, name that God revealed to Moses (Exodus 3:15). Thus, the Spirit of the Lord is the Spirit of the one true God who chose Israel and revealed himself to them. Moreover, throughout Scripture He is the one who executes God's mission in the earth. Every action of the Spirit described in Scripture is initiated from the purpose and mission of God the Father.

Spirit of Jesus Christ

The New Testament also reveals the Holy Spirit to be the *Spirit of Jesus Christ*. Twice He is called the "Spirit of Christ" (Romans 8:9; 1 Peter 1:11), and once He is called the "Spirit of Jesus" (Acts 16:7). He is also referred to as the "Spirit of Jesus Christ" (Philippians 1:19), and in a passage that refers to Jesus as being God's Son, He is called the "Spirit of his Son" (Galatians 4:4–6).

Jesus promised that He would not leave the disciples as orphans but would come to them and remain with them forever. He would do this through the presence of the Holy Spirit (John 14:16–18). When Christ returned to heaven, the Spirit of Christ came to continue Christ's work through the church (15:26–27; 16:7–8). The Spirit of Christ fills and empowers us to fulfill the mission that Christ began.

Paraclete

The term *Paraclete* is a name for the Holy Spirit that is found only in the writings of John and comes from the Greek word *Paraklētos*. This word means "one who is called on to provide guidance, encouragement, and enablement." During the Last Supper, Jesus used this name four times in referring to the Holy Spirit (John 14:16, 26; 15:26; 16:7). Some have translated the word *Paraklētos* inadequately as "Comforter." More recent translations translate it as "Helper," "Counselor," or "Advocate."

In his first epistle, John refers to Jesus as the Paraclete (1 John 2:1). However, on the night before His death Jesus promised to send the Holy Spirit as another Paraclete like himself who would take His place (John 14:16).

Jesus taught and trained His disciples (Matthew 11:1). He also sent them out to proclaim the good news of the kingdom of God and gave them authority to heal the sick and cast out demonic spirits (10:1, 7–8). Then, before returning to heaven, He gave His disciples the same mission the Father had given Him (John 20:21). Moreover, He promised them another Helper to take His place and enable them for that mission. This same Holy Spirit is now present with us as a Paraclete to teach and to guide us (14:26) and to enable us to carry out God's mission (Acts 1:8).

Spirit of Truth

Spirit of Truth is the second name for the Holy Spirit found only in the writings of John. During the Last Supper, Jesus referred to the Holy Spirit as the Spirit of Truth three times (John 14:17; 15:26;

16:13). He promised, "When he, the Spirit of truth, comes, he will guide you into all the truth" (16:13), and "he will testify about me" (15:26). Jesus then commanded His disciples to join the Spirit of Truth in testifying about Him (15:27).

John later wrote that the Spirit testifies about Jesus *"because the Spirit is the truth"* (1 John 5:6, emphasis added). John further declared that one's confession of Christ is the ultimate test of whether that person has the Spirit of Truth or another spirit that is not from God (4:2–3, 6).

The world has been deceived by the lies of Satan and is in slavery to sin (John 8:34, 44). Jesus Christ is the truth that sets people free from that sin (8:31–32; 14:6). The Spirit of Truth continues to testify the truth about Jesus to the world so that it might be set free. As Christ's disciples, we are called to join the Holy Spirit in proclaiming the truth of the gospel to the lost and setting them free from the bondage of sin.

Other Names and Titles

Several other names for the Holy Spirit appear only once or twice in the Bible. These names are also significant and add to our understanding of the Spirit and His work.

Isaiah listed six names for the Holy Spirit (Isaiah 11:2). He declared that the Spirit of the Lord would rest on the Messiah, empowering Him to establish the kingdom of God. He gave six names for the Spirit that describe how the Spirit would empower the Messiah to fulfill His mission:

- The Spirit of wisdom
- The Spirit of understanding
- The Spirit of counsel
- The Spirit of might
- The Spirit of knowledge

- The Spirit of the fear of the LORD

The author of Hebrews speaks of the *eternal Spirit* who enabled Christ to offer himself as the perfect sacrifice for our sins on the cross (Hebrews 9:14). The author also refers to the Holy Spirit as the "Spirit of grace" (10:29).

In Romans, Paul mentions two more names for the Holy Spirit. Both point to the Spirit's work in the mission of God. He refers to the Holy Spirit as the *Spirit of life* (8:2) and the *Spirit of sonship* (8:15). The Holy Spirit is thus the one who takes people who are dead in transgressions and sins and brings them to life in Christ (Ephesians 2:1–5). Just as the Holy Spirit was involved in breathing life into man at creation (Genesis 2:7), He is also involved in breathing the life of God back into lost sinners and transforming them into sons and daughters of God (John 1:12–13; 3:3–6).

SYMBOLS OF THE HOLY SPIRIT

The Bible often uses symbols to help us understand its message. Biblical symbols are not sources of spiritual power. They are given to teach us by analogy. Analogy is noting certain qualities found in one thing that apply to another. Pay close attention to the ways in which symbols of the Spirit reveal His qualities and His work in God's mission.

Breath, Air, Wind

The Bible frequently uses the related elements of breath, air, and wind to symbolize the Holy Spirit. In fact, the word for *spirit* in Hebrew *(ruach)* and Greek *(pneuma)* can be variously translated as "spirit," "breath," "air," or "wind" in both languages, depending on the context. This group of related symbols primarily point to the active power of the Holy Spirit. They are also connected to the Spirit's life-giving power, both physical and spiritual. Job declared,

"The Spirit of God has made me; the breath of the Almighty gives me life" (Job 33:4)

God showed Ezekiel the life-giving power of the Spirit in a vision of a valley of dry bones (Ezekiel 37:1–14). The bones represented a spiritually dead Israel whom God promised to bring back to life through the wind and breath of His Spirit. Jesus likewise revealed the dynamic, life-giving power of the Spirit through the symbol of wind (John 3:5–8).

This dynamic power of the Spirit symbolized by wind is also connected to the participation of God's people in His mission. On the Day of Pentecost, when God poured out His Spirit, the first manifestation of the Spirit was the sound of a powerful wind that came from heaven (Acts 2:2). Jesus had promised the disciples that they would be baptized in the Holy Spirit and empowered as His witnesses (1:4–5, 8). The sound of wind was one of the evidences that what was happening was the fulfillment of Jesus' promise to baptize the disciples with the Holy Spirit and empower them for God's mission. One might say that on the Day of Pentecost, God blew on His church to empower it by His Spirit to witness about His desire to breathe life back into all who are dead in sin.

Fire

Fire is a symbol of the Holy Spirit that points to His work of inspiring prophetic speech. As such, it has important missional significance for the Spirit's work of empowering believers for witness (Acts 1:8).

On the Day of Pentecost, when God poured out His Spirit out on the church, a tongue of fire came to rest on each of the believers (Acts 2:3). They were then filled with the Spirit and began to speak in different languages as the Spirit enabled them (2:4). The tongues of fire symbolized the Holy Spirit, who put God's words in the disciples' mouths. Peter later explained what happened by quoting

Joel's prophesy that God would pour out His Spirit, and as a result, His people would prophesy (2:17–18; ref. Joel 2:28).

The Old Testament also connects fire to the word of God that the Spirit inspired the prophets to proclaim. God told Jeremiah, "I will make my words in your mouth a fire" (Jeremiah 5:14, see also 23:29). Jeremiah himself declared that God's word "is in my heart like a fire, a fire shut up in my bones" (Jeremiah 20:9). In the New Testament, Paul connected fire to the Spirit's work of inspiring prophecy when he warned the Thessalonians: "Do not quench the Spirit. Do not treat prophecies with contempt" (1 Thessalonians 5:19–20). Today the Holy Spirit empowers and inspires believers to proclaim the gospel to the lost (Acts 4:31).

Water

In the Bible, water is also often used as a symbol of the Holy Spirit. Water represents the refreshing, renewing, and life-giving work of the Spirit that satisfies the thirst of our hearts.

Isaiah used water as a symbol of the Spirit to announce God's promise: "I will pour water on the thirsty land, and streams on the dry ground; I will pour out my Spirit on your offspring, and my blessing on your descendants" (Isaiah 44:3). Jesus likewise used water as a symbol of the Holy Spirit. He invited all who were thirsty to come to Him and drink. He promised that He would give them the "living water" of the Holy Spirit (John 4:10).

The symbol of water also has important missional significance. Jesus declared that not only would the Holy Spirit *be in us* to satisfy the longing of our hearts, but He would also become a river of living water *flowing out of us* to give life to others (John 7:38). This analogy depicts how the Spirit enables us to share the blessings of God with others.

Oil

Oil is yet another symbol of the Holy Spirit that points to how the Spirit enables God's people to participate in His mission. When Israel was attempting to rebuild their temple, which had been destroyed by the Babylonians, Zechariah received a vision from God. In the vision, he saw a lampstand and a bowl supplying oil to keep the lamp burning (Zechariah 4:1–2). When Zechariah asked about the meaning of the vision, God told him that the work would be accomplished "not by might nor by power, but by my Spirit" (4:6). It is the Spirit of God who gives us the ability to do God's work.

The Old Testament also correlates anointing a person with oil to the empowering presence of the Spirit. This is most clearly seen in the life of King David (1 Samuel 16:13; see also Saul's anointing in 10:1, 6, 10).

Based on this symbolic use of anointing oil in the Old Testament, the New Testament speaks of anointing when it refers to the Spirit's empowering of God's servants. Jesus is the ideal example of one who was anointed with the Holy Spirit for God's mission. Jesus began and described His ministry by quoting from the prophet Isaiah: "The Spirit of the Lord is on me, because he has anointed me to proclaim the good news to the poor. He has sent me to proclaim freedom for the prisoners and recovery of sight for the blind, to set the oppressed free, to proclaim the year of the Lord's favor" (Luke 4:18–19; compare Isaiah 61:1–2). Peter later declared, "God anointed Jesus of Nazareth with the Holy Spirit and power and…he went around doing good and healing all who were under the power of the devil" (Acts 10:38).

Since Pentecost, all believers can be anointed with and empowered by the Holy Spirit for missional service. Paul wrote that God has "anointed us,…and put his Spirit in our hearts" (2 Corinthians 1:21–22). John declared that we "have an anointing from the Holy One" (1 John 2:20, 27).

The Hand/Finger/Arm of God

The Holy Spirit is also often symbolized by the finger, hand, or arm of God. This symbol points to the powerful and miraculous works of the Holy Spirit to advance God's mission. For example, this symbol is used repeatedly to refer to the powerful works God performed when He delivered Israel from slavery in Egypt (Deuteronomy 4:34, 37; 5:15). The prophets also used this as a symbol of the Holy Spirit coming on them in power to reveal God's word to them. Isaiah testified, "This is what the LORD says to me with his strong hand upon me" (Isaiah 8:11). Jeremiah also used the hand of the Lord as a symbol of the Spirit coming on him to reveal God's word to him (Jeremiah 15:16–17). Ezekiel often used this symbol, and in three instances he clearly identified the hand of the Lord on him as being the Spirit of God (Ezekiel 3:14; 8:3; 37:1).

The New Testament uses this same symbol to refer to the Holy Spirit and His powerful work in advancing God's mission. Jesus declared, "If I drive out demons by the finger of God, then the kingdom of God has come upon you" (Luke 11:20). In Matthew's parallel passage, Jesus reveals the finger of God to be the Spirit of God (Matthew 12:28).

Seal

In his epistles, Paul uses a seal as a symbol of the Holy Spirit (2 Corinthians 1:21–22; Ephesians 1:13; 4:30). In New Testament times, a seal was used on important documents and other items to verify the identity of the genuine owner. As God's seal on our lives, the presence of the Holy Spirit proves we belong to God and guarantees that we are recipients of God's blessing and salvation.

Dove

Each of the four Gospels uses a dove to symbolize the Holy Spirit's work in enabling Jesus to perform His ministry. Jesus began

His ministry at His baptism. At that moment "the Holy Spirit descended on him in bodily form like a dove" (Luke 3:22–23; see also Matthew 3:16; Mark 1:10; John 1:32). Under the Law, people sometimes offered a dove to God to make atonement for sin (Leviticus 12:6). The dove coming to rest on Jesus symbolized the work of the Spirit in empowering Him to accomplish His redemptive mission (see Luke 4:17–18).

IMPLICATIONS AND APPLICATIONS

In this lesson, we have examined many Scriptures that reveal who the Holy Spirit is. We have demonstrated that He is a divine person and is, in fact, God. These are more than just truths to be recognized. They have profound implications for our lives and our service in God's mission.

Because the Holy Spirit is God, we can trust Him and follow His leading with confidence. He knows everything, which means He will make no mistakes as He leads us into God's mission. He is all-powerful and able to accomplish every good thing God intends to do in and through our lives. The Holy Spirit is omnipresent and will never leave us on our own. He is holy and pure, and therefore, we should obey Him and ask Him to help us live holy lives that please God and adequately represent Him and His character to a lost and dying world.

The fact that the Holy Spirit is a person also has great implications for us. The Holy Spirit is not an impersonal force but a person we can know and relate to. He knows us and loves us, and we can know and love Him. We can speak to Him in prayer, and He will speak to us and teach us everything we need to know about God and His will. He will even help us pray more effectively. No Christian ever needs to feel that they are alone. The Holy Spirit is ready and waiting for us to invite Him into our lives so we can enjoy fellowship with Him and receive His power.

Chapter 2 ~ The Holy Spirit: A Divine Person

It is not enough, however, to recognize that the Holy Spirit is a divine Person. To know and appreciate Him, we must also understand that He is "God's missionary Spirit." In these last days, God has poured out His Spirit to empower the church to fulfill His mission to redeem the nations (Acts 1:8; 2:17–21). Consequently, He works through us to carry out God's mission of saving the world from sin. In this chapter, we saw this truth reflected repeatedly in the names and symbols of the Holy Spirit. We must now commit ourselves to join Him in this vital work of testifying to the truth about Christ. If we will make this commitment, the Holy Spirit will anoint us and empower us just as He anointed and empowered Jesus and the early church. In the next chapter, we will examine the mission of God and the role the Holy Spirits plays in fulfilling that mission.

Chapter 2 ~ The Holy Spirit: A Divine Person

Questions for Discussion and Reflection

1. How would you explain the concept of the Trinity to a new believer?

2. Since the Holy Spirit is a person, how can we help believers develop a relationship with Him?

3. What do we learn about the missionary nature of the Holy Spirit from the study of His names?

4. What do we learn about the missionary nature of the Holy Spirit from the study of the symbols of the Holy Spirit?

~ CHAPTER 3 ~

THE HOLY SPIRIT:
A MISSIONARY SPIRIT

Understanding the mission of God is an important key to rightly interpreting Scripture. Assemblies of God missionary and author John York wrote, "Since God has always had a mission, the Bible should be read missiologically."[7] Indeed, the Bible reveals that God is on a mission to create for himself a holy people from all the peoples of the earth. Scholars call this work of God the *missio Dei*. *Missio Dei* is a Latin term meaning "mission of God." Missiologist David Hesselgrave argues, "The missionary purpose of God is…so interwoven with the entire fabric of God's plan as revealed in the Bible that it becomes a pre-understanding for the interpretation of the whole Bible."[8] This missiological perspective on Scripture naturally impacts our study of the Holy Spirit.

---

[7] John V. York, *Missions in the Age of the Spirit* (Springfield, MO: Logion Press, 2000), 20.

[8] David J. Hesselgrave, "A Missionary Hermeneutic : Understanding Scripture in the Light of World Mission," *International Journal of Frontier Missions* 10, no. 1 (January 1, 1993): 17.

Chapter 3 – The Holy Spirit: A Missionary Spirit

READING THE BIBLE MISSIOLOGICALLY

Jesus' words to His disciples following His resurrection demonstrate the importance of reading the Bible missiologically:

> He said to them, "How foolish you are, and how slow to believe all that the prophets have spoken! Did not the Messiah have to suffer these things and then enter his glory?" *And beginning with Moses and all the Prophets, he explained to them what was said in all the Scriptures concerning himself.* (Luke 24:25–27, emphasis added)

Jesus further stated:

> "This is what I told you while I was still with you: Everything must be fulfilled that is written about me in the Law of Moses, the Prophets and the Psalms." Then he opened their minds so they could understand the Scriptures. He told them, "This is what is written: The Messiah will suffer and rise from the dead on the third day, *and repentance for the forgiveness of sins will be preached in his name to all nations, beginning at Jerusalem. You are witnesses of these things. I am going to send you what my Father has promised; but stay in the city until you have been clothed with power from on high.*" (Luke 24:44–49, emphasis added)

Notice how in these verses, Jesus "explained to them what was said in all the Scriptures concerning himself." In other words, He showed them how the entire Old Testament finds its focus and fulfillment in His life, death, resurrection, and subsequent mission to all nations. When we interpret the Bible in light of God's mission to save the world through Christ, we interpret it as it was intended to be interpreted.

The Empowering Missionary Spirit

What Jesus said in Luke 24:46–49 is especially important for our present study. His words directly link the missional focus of Scripture to the empowering work of the Holy Spirit. After announcing that "repentance for the forgiveness of sins will be preached in his name to all nations, beginning at Jerusalem," Jesus informed His disciples that they were "witnesses of these things." He then commanded them to "stay in the city until [they had] been clothed with power from on high" (Luke 24:46–49). Verse 49 is a clear reference to being empowered by the Holy Spirit (compare Acts 1:4–5, 8).

Christ connected the person and work of the Spirit to the fulfillment of His mission. In other words, we can fulfill our God-given role in missions only as we collaborate with and are empowered by God's missionary Spirit. It is important for us to remember that God's mission and the Holy Spirit's mission are the same.

Chapter Overview

In this chapter, we will discover how the Holy Spirit is indeed the Spirit of Missions. We will begin by briefly surveying the entire Bible to point out its interwoven missiological and pneumatological emphasis. Then we will examine how the Bible is itself a product of God's mission. The Holy Spirit inspired the Scriptures in order that people might know God and be reconciled to Him. While it is true that the Bible is the basis for missions, we will also learn that God's mission is the basis for the Bible.

THE HOLY SPIRIT: THE SPIRIT OF MISSIONS

From beginning to end, the Bible depicts the Holy Spirit as working to accomplish the *missio Dei* (mission of God). Let us take a brief survey of Scripture to see this.

The Missionary Spirit in Creation

The book of Genesis reveals that the Holy Spirit was active in the creation of both the world and humankind (Genesis 1:2; 2:7; compare Job 34:14–15; Psalm 104:30). By creating the world and then creating people in His own image, God, through the Holy Spirit, began to execute His mission in the earth. He was creating a people for himself, and the Holy Spirit was there executing God's mission. Thus, the Holy Spirit participated in God's mission from the very beginning of creation.

Later, when Adam and Eve sinned against God, they opened the door to evil and death in the world. This act, however, did not change God's mission, nor did it stop Him from carrying it out. And, as we shall see, the Holy Spirit has been there every step of the way.

The Missionary Spirit and Israel

God worked by His Spirit to establish the nation of Israel as His special people. He did this by calling and blessing Abraham (Genesis 12:1–3) and by anointing prophets and leaders with His Spirit to guide and prepare the nation. His intention was to work through Abraham's descendants to make the way for all nations to be blessed (Galatians 3:8, 14–16). We will discuss this more in Chapters 4 and 5 where we talk about the work of the Holy Spirit in advancing God's mission in the Old Testament.

The Missionary Spirit in Christ

The missionary work of the Spirit that began in the Old Testament continued in the New Testament. In the Gospels and Acts, the Spirit worked in and through the ministries of Jesus, the apostles, and the early believers to advance the *missio Dei.*

Jesus began His ministry at His baptism only after "the Holy Spirit descended on him in bodily form like a dove" (Luke 3:22–23). He then announced, "The Spirit of the Lord is on me, because he has anointed me to proclaim good news" (4:18). In Peter's sermon in Caesarea, he summarized Jesus' Spirit-empowered ministry like this: "God anointed Jesus of Nazareth with the Holy Spirit and power, and...he went around doing good and healing all who were under the power of the devil, because God was with him" (Acts 10:38).

The Missionary Spirit and the Great Commission

During His ministry on earth, Jesus also called disciples to join Him in His Father's mission. Later, during the forty days between His resurrection and ascension, He commanded them to "go and make disciples of all nations...teaching them to obey everything I have commanded you" (Matthew 28:18–20; compare Mark 16:20; Luke 24:46–48; John 20:21–22; and Acts 1:8). This command is known as the Great Commission. Every disciple of Christ should recognize that they are also called and commissioned by Christ to join Him in this mission.

It is further significant that every time Jesus issued His Great Commission, He included a promise of His power or presence:

- "And surely I am with you always, to the very end of the age" (Matthew 28:20).
- "And these signs will accompany those who believe" (Mark 16:17).
- "You [will be] clothed with power from on high" (Luke 24:49).
- "He breathed on them and said, 'Receive the Holy Spirit'" (John 20:22).
- "You will receive power when the Holy Spirit comes on you" (Acts 1:8).

In each of these instances, the source of divine enablement is the Holy Spirit. This promise of power is for every disciple who joins Jesus in His mission.

The Missionary Spirit in the Book of Acts

The book of Acts presents the Holy Spirit as the dynamic force behind the astounding missionary success of the early church. By being baptized in the Holy Spirit, the followers of Jesus were transformed into God's Spirit-empowered missionary people. When the Spirit came on them at Pentecost (and many times afterward), they were given the power they needed to become effective witnesses for Christ, as He had promised in Acts 1:8. Throughout Acts, every time the Spirit is poured out, the result is missional witness (compare Acts 2:1–42; 4:31–33; 9:17–20; 13:1–4; 19:1–10).

The Missionary Spirit in the New Testament Epistles

The New Testament Epistles often highlight the work of the Spirit in sanctifying and transforming God's people into a holy temple in which He may dwell now and forever (Ephesians 2:19–22). The Epistles also present the Spirit as the one who inspires and empowers missions. In his first letter to the church in Corinth, Paul reminded the believers there that when he had come to them, he had come "with a demonstration of the Spirit's power, so that [their] faith might not rest on human wisdom, but on God's power" (1 Corinthians 2:4–5). To the Thessalonians he wrote, "Our gospel came to you not simply with words but also with power, with the Holy Spirit and deep conviction" (1 Thessalonians 1:5). Finally, Paul testified to the Roman church that God had used him to lead the Gentiles to obey God "by the power of signs and wonders, through the power of the Spirit of God" (Romans 15:18–19). The empowering work of the Holy Spirit was at the core of Paul's missionary strategy.

The Missionary Spirit in the Book of Revelation

The book of Revelation tells the dramatic story of God completing His mission on earth. From the beginning, when God first created Adam and Eve in the Garden, His plan has been to fashion a people for himself that He might be with them forever (Revelation 21:3). Until Christ returns at the end of the age, the Spirit will continue this work through the church. This shared missionary desire of God, the Spirit, and the church is displayed in the concluding verses of the Bible:

> The Spirit and the bride [the church] say, "Come!" And let the one who hears say, "Come!" Let the one who is thirsty come; and let the one who wishes take the free gift of the water of life. (Revelation 22:17)

"Come to Jesus" is the passionate cry of the church that is empowered and inspired by the missionary Spirit. The church extends this glorious invitation to every generation until Jesus returns. Only then will its mission be complete.

The Missionary Spirit Today

Because He is by nature a missionary Spirit, the Holy Spirit continues to propel the church forward in mission, just as He did in Scripture. Today, God sends His Spirit to transform His people into a missionary people. Each time one of God's people is filled with the Spirit, that person is empowered for God's mission. The Spirit then propels the person into God's harvest field. God transforms and empowers His people so they might join Him in His mission of creating a people for himself "from every tribe and language and people and nation" (Revelation 5:9).

In our study of the person and work of the Holy Spirit, we must recognize that the Holy Spirit is indeed the Spirit of Missions.

Scripture reveals a vital connection between the work of the Spirit and the fulfillment of God's redemptive mission. By the time we finish this study, we will all agree that the work of the Spirit is at the heart of God's mission to redeem and transform humanity. He is truly God's missionary Spirit.

THE MISSIONARY SPIRIT: THE INSPIRER OF SCRIPTURE

One amazing missionary work of the Holy Spirit is the revelation of Scripture. The Bible is like no other book. It consists of sixty-six books written by approximately forty authors from a wide variety of backgrounds. Among them were kings, shepherds, farmers, fishermen, doctors, soldiers, politicians, and rabbis. They lived over a period of more than 1,500 years and wrote from various locations using different languages and various styles of writing. However, within its diversity, the Bible is one book with one central message. It reveals God's mission to redeem humanity and prepare a people for himself.

How is this amazing unity possible? It is the result of the work of the Holy Spirit. While many people were involved in writing the Bible, the Holy Spirit inspired and guided them all in what they wrote. As a result, the Holy Spirit is the real author of the Bible and the source of its message.

The work of the Spirit in inspiring the Scriptures is a fundamental aspect of His missionary work. The very existence of the Bible is a clear declaration that God is a missionary God and the Holy Spirit is a missionary Spirit. In other words, God gave us the Bible because He wants people to know and serve Him. Throughout history, the Holy Spirit has worked through the prophets and apostles, revealing God's word to and through them. He has done this so that people might know God and His will for their lives. The Holy Spirit wants all people to know God and be reconciled to Him through faith in Christ.

As such, the Bible is more than just a record of God's words and works in history. It plays an essential role in the mission of God. When the Spirit revealed God's word through the prophets, it was a missionary action designed to advance the plan of salvation. God was intent on completing His mission.

The Bible's Claim of Inspiration

The Bible claims to be inspired by the Holy Spirit. Paul wrote that "all Scripture is God-breathed" (2 Timothy 3:16). He was saying that the Holy Spirit inspired the entire Bible. This image of Scripture being God-breathed makes us think of how God created Adam. God "breathed into his nostrils the breath of life, and man became a living being" (Genesis 2:7). The same Spirit who breathed life into man breathed out God's life-giving word to mankind. No wonder Jesus declared that "man shall not live on bread alone, but on every word that comes from the mouth of God" (Matthew 4:4).

Peter described in more detail how the Spirit inspired those who wrote the Scriptures: "Above all, you must understand that no prophecy of Scripture came about by the prophet's own interpretation of things. For prophecy never had its origin in the human will, but prophets, though human, spoke from God as they were carried along by the Holy Spirit" (2 Peter 1:20–21). Citing this text, Anthony Palma wrote, "One may say that God is the source of Scripture, the Holy Spirit is the agent by whom the Scriptures were given, and people are the instruments who, under the guidance of the Spirit, wrote the Scriptures."[9]

Other biblical passages testify how the Spirit inspired the Bible. When quoting an Old Testament passage, the writer of Hebrews often began with the phrase "as the Holy Spirit says" (Hebrews 3:7; compare 9:8; 10:15). Jesus also affirmed the divine origin of the

---

[9] Anthony D. Palma, *The Holy Spirit: A Pentecostal Perspective* (Springfield, MO: Logion Press, 2001), 82.

Scriptures—as well as the role of the Spirit in inspiring them (Mark 7:6–13; 12:36).

All the New Testament authors recognized that the Spirit inspired what they wrote. For example, Jesus claimed that the words He spoke were inspired by the Spirit and came from God (Luke 4:18–19; John 3:34; 6:63; Acts 1:2). Paul also considered the words he wrote to be inspired by the Spirit. He told the Corinthians, "This is what we speak, not in words taught us by human wisdom but in words taught by the Spirit" (1 Corinthians 2:13; compare 2:16). Peter supported Paul's claim of divine inspiration, and placed Paul's letters on the same level as other Scriptures. He said that Paul "wrote you with the wisdom that God gave him" and referred to Paul's letters as "Scriptures" (2 Peter 3:15–16). In like manner, John portrayed the entire book of Revelation as being inspired by the Holy Spirit (Revelation 1:10; 2:7, 11, 17, 29; 3:6, 13, 22; 4:2; 22:17).

Important Terms Defined

Theologians sometimes use the terms *revelation, inspiration,* and *illumination* to describe the work of the Holy Spirit in inspiring Scripture. It is important that we carefully define each of these terms. This will help us to clearly understand the missional work of the Spirit in producing the Bible.

Revelation

To *reveal* something is to uncover it. It means to make something known that was previously hidden or unknown. In theology, we sometimes use the noun form of the word, *revelation,* to refer to the complete Bible. The Bible is God's revelation of himself to people.

This, of course, does not mean that everything recorded in the Bible was unknown to the authors before God revealed it to them. For example, there are historical events that were well known to the authors and their readers. At times, they were even eyewitnesses to these events. What happened, however, was that the Holy Spirit revealed to them the meaning of these events as they relate to God's plan and His purposes for humanity.

Through disobedience, humanity lost a relationship with God (Romans 1:21–23). They not only lost their relationship with God, but they also lost much of their knowledge and understanding of Him (1 Corinthians 1:18–21; 2:14). Nevertheless, God in His great mercy took the initiative to reveal himself to humanity. He did this through His words and actions, which He has recorded for us in the Bible through the Holy Spirit. In its pages, we discover many things we would never have known otherwise.

For example, through the Holy Spirit, God revealed to the prophets His messages for the nation of Israel, and the prophets wrote down these messages (Zechariah 7:12). In the New Testament, God gave the book of Revelation to the apostle John in a vision from the Holy Spirit (Revelation 1:10; 4:2; 17:3; 21:10; 22:17). Paul spoke of the gospel—the message of salvation through faith in Christ—as a great mystery that was hidden in times past but now has been "revealed to us by his Spirit" (1 Corinthians 2:7–10; compare Ephesians 3:3–5).

Inspiration

Inspiration describes the role of the Spirit in guiding the production of the Scriptures. We have examined certain passages that affirm the role of the Holy Spirit as the one who inspired Scripture. We should know, however, that there are various theories concerning the level of the Spirit's involvement in the process.

Some Bible scholars argue that while the Holy Spirit may have guided the production of the Bible, there are elements in the Bible that are purely the product of the writers. This has led them to conclude incorrectly that the Bible *contains* God's word but is not *entirely* God's word. This idea has led to many fruitless arguments over which parts of the Bible are divinely inspired and which are not. We must flatly reject this theory of partial inspiration.

At the other extreme, some people have suggested that the Holy Spirit literally dictated every word recorded in the Bible in the same way that someone would dictate a letter word for word to a secretary. This concept implies that there is no trace of human involvement in the wording of the Bible. However, this idea does not match up with many of the characteristics found in the Bible, such as the variety of vocabulary and writing styles used by the authors.

The best explanation is a concept called *verbal plenary inspiration*. The word *verbal* indicates that the Holy Spirit inspired the very words found in Scripture. He did not dictate every word, but He carefully guided the authors in their choice of wording. The word *plenary* indicates that the Holy Spirit fully inspired the entire Bible.

The idea of verbal plenary inspiration recognizes both the human author's personality and writing style and the Spirit's oversight in the production of Scripture. It was a process whereby the Holy Spirit guided and superintended the authors as they wrote. They wrote using their own vocabulary and style, but the Holy Spirit inspired and directed the content of what they wrote. As a result, the words they wrote accurately and completely express the message God intended to communicate. The entire Bible is God's Word, His powerful life-giving Word that can bring people to salvation through faith in Christ (2 Timothy 3:15–17; 1 Peter 1:20–21).

Illumination

Another missional work of the Spirit in relation to Scripture is *illumination*. To illuminate something is to shine a light on it so that it becomes more clearly visible. The term is sometimes used figuratively. In this sense, it means to make an idea clearer and easier to understand. As the Spirit of Missions, the Holy Spirit wants people to understand the message of the Bible and be saved. Therefore, He works to illuminate the meaning of the text to the minds of all who sincerely seek after God. He helps them understand, accept, and apply the Word of God to their lives. This, then, is another ongoing activity of the Spirit—illuminating Scripture. He does this for both unsaved and saved people.

Illumination and the unsaved. In his letters, Paul described sinful people as being "darkened in their understanding and separated from the life of God" (Ephesians 4:18; compare Romans 1:21). Consequently, they are unable to understand spiritual realities and the truth about God (1 Corinthians 2:14). The apostle explained the reason why: "The god of this age [the devil] has blinded the minds of unbelievers, so that they cannot see the light of the gospel" (2 Corinthians 4:4). He wrote further, "The person without the Spirit does not accept the things that come from the Spirit of God but considers them foolishness, and cannot understand them because they are discerned only through the Spirit" (1 Corinthians 2:14). Therefore, without the help of the Spirit, it is impossible for an unsaved person to understand and accept the truth of the Bible. Paul reminded Timothy, his son in the faith, that the Scriptures "are able to make you wise for salvation through faith in Christ Jesus" (2 Timothy 3:15). Thus, the unsaved need the Spirit of Truth to illuminate their minds and open their hearts to believe the truth of the gospel and accept Christ as Savior (John 15:26).

Illumination and the saved. Even after people come to faith in Christ, they continue to need the Spirit's illumination. They need Him to illuminate God's Word to their mind and apply its teachings to their heart. The Holy Spirit is the divine author and inspirer of Scripture. It is therefore reasonable to assume that He is its best interpreter. As the Spirit of Truth, He alone can lead us into the full understanding of God's truth (John 16:13).

Paul prayed for the Ephesians: "I keep asking that the God of our Lord Jesus Christ, the glorious Father, may give you the Spirit of wisdom and revelation, so that you may know him better. I pray that the eyes of your heart may be enlightened" (Ephesians 1:17–18). Like Paul, we should continually ask God to give us His Spirit to open our minds to better understand and apply the truths found in His Word. The mission of the Holy Spirit is not just to lead sinners to believe in Christ; it is also to enlighten and transform believers into the image of Christ (2 Corinthians 3:18).

A warning is in order here. We must remember that the truth the Holy Spirit helps us understand is the truth contained in the Bible. In this sense, the Spirit's work of illumination is distinct from His work of revelation. In illuminating Scripture to us, the Spirit is in no sense revealing new truth apart from the Bible. He is also not revealing mysterious or hidden meanings in the Bible that no one else is capable of understanding. The truth is in God's Word, but we need the Holy Spirit to help us see it and properly understand it.

We also need the Spirit's help to see how the Word applies to our individual lives. We need His illumination to make us conscious of what He is saying to us personally through His Word. The Word of God is alive and so powerful that it can penetrate every part of our being, revealing and judging even our deepest thoughts and the attitudes of our hearts (Hebrews 4:12). As we study the Bible, the Holy Spirit is present and ready to make the Word of God come alive in our hearts and minds. What a wonderful and transforming experience it is to sense the presence of the Spirit as we reflect on God's Word and realize that He is speaking directly to our real and present needs.

The Spirit and the Word

As Pentecostals, we believe that God continues to speak to us today by His Spirit. Later in our study, we will look at the prophetic gifts of the Spirit that are so vital for the church and for the advancement of God's mission in the world. Right now, it is important that we consider how a prophetic word spoken by the inspiration of the Spirit today relates to the word of God as recorded in the Bible.

In short, we must flatly reject any "prophetic word" that is not in full agreement with what is written in the Bible. No teaching, revelation, or Spirit-inspired prophecy given today can ever be considered superior in authority to (or even equal to) what is recorded in the Bible. The Bible is God's eternal, inspired Word. Pentecostals believe and teach that "the Scriptures, both the Old and New Testaments, are verbally inspired of God and are the revelation of God to man, the infallible, authoritative rule of faith and conduct."[10]

The writer of Hebrews tells us that God revealed His Word through the prophets, but now in these last days, He has spoken to us by His Son, Jesus Christ (Hebrews 1:1–2). In other words, the Spirit spoke through the Hebrew prophets and the New Testament apostles and eyewitnesses of Christ's ministry to produce a final and complete revelation of God's eternal Word. The Bible thus provides humanity with an unchanging, objective standard by which we must measure all other messages. God's Word is forever (Psalm 119:89). Today, any genuinely Spirit-inspired prophetic message will always support and agree with the message of Scripture.

Further, we must remember the repeated warnings of Jesus and the apostles, who said that false prophets would appear claiming to speak by the Spirit. As a result, these false prophets would lead many people astray (Matthew 7:15, 22–23; 2 Peter 2:1–3; 1 John 4:1). Because of this, we must carefully judge all prophetic messages to determine whether they are genuinely from the Spirit of God. John warned, "Do not believe every spirit, but test the spirits to see whether they are from God, because many false prophets have gone out into the world" (1 John 4:1). Paul similarly advised that when

---

[10] "Statement of Fundamental Truths," in *Constitution of the General Council of the Assemblies of God, revised August 2017* (General Council of the Assemblies of God, USA, 2017), p. 121

prophetic words are given, the church should carefully evaluate what is said (1 Corinthians 14:29). Using the Bible as our God-given objective standard, and relying on the Holy Spirit to guide us in our understanding of the Bible, we can discern which messages are from God and which ones are not (1 Timothy 6:3–4; 2 Timothy 1:13–14; 3:14–17; 4:1–4).

Remaining in the Truth

In order to remain in God's truth as revealed in Scripture, we must employ two important strategies. First, we must remain full of the Spirit and submitted to the will of God. In doing this, we will humbly depend on the Spirit to guide us and alert us to false teachings. The Bible tells us that false prophecies and "things taught by demons" are attractive to those who live according to the sinful nature (1 Timothy 4:1). However, those who walk in the Spirit depend on the Spirit of Truth to lead them into truth (John 14:26; 16:13). Second, we must diligently study the Word of God. The people of Berea are a good example of this kind of approach. The Bible says that the Bereans were of such noble character that they received Paul's message with eagerness, and they "examined the Scriptures every day to see if what Paul said was true" (Acts 17:11).

Never forget that the Spirit of God and the Word of God always work in complete harmony. The Holy Spirit who revealed and inspired God's Word will never contradict, change, or add to what He has previously revealed. This is why every follower of Jesus Christ must know and understand the Bible. Such knowledge will equip the believer to rightly judge the truth or error of prophetic words. The promise that the Holy Spirit will lead us into truth is no substitute for studying the Scriptures. Today, the Spirit of God continues to speak through anointed preaching and teaching and through prophetic words. However, all these methods must work together to confirm what has already been revealed and written in God's Word.

IMPLICATIONS AND APPLICATIONS

Two powerful implications flow from our understanding of the Holy Spirit as God's missionary Spirit. The first is that a true people of the Spirit will always be a missionary people. The second is that a true people of the Spirit will always be a people of the Word. Let us look at each of these implications.

A Missionary People

Because of their experience with God's missionary Spirit, people of the Spirit will always be missionary people. We began this chapter by discussing the importance of God's mission as the necessary context for understanding the Bible's teaching concerning the Holy Spirit. We also discussed how the whole Bible presents the Holy Spirit as continually working to accomplish God's mission. His missionary role is so central to the Bible's presentation of the Spirit that we must conclude He is by nature a missionary Spirit.

This truth has great implications for us today. If God's missionary Spirit indwells us and we have been truly empowered by the Spirit, then we should, by nature, be a missionary people. When we find Pentecostal believers who are not actively participating in evangelism, church planting, and missions, this should give us cause for concern. It should motivate us to examine what is wrong and to seek again to be a missionary people of the Spirit.

The book of Acts presents the Holy Spirit as the Superintendent of the Harvest. This means He was the one who directed the apostles and early disciples where to go, and He showed them what to do in carrying out their ministries. He did this for Philip (Acts 8:29), Peter (10:9), Paul (16:7), and others. He wants to do the same for us today.

This is why we should always seek to follow the Spirit's leading and commit ourselves to work with Him in God's mission. God's missionary Spirit is ready to empower, direct, and sustain us in the work. Therefore, we must seek to remain full of His Spirit and stay obedient to His command to witness for Christ "in Jerusalem, and in all Judea and Samaria, and to the ends of the earth" (Acts 1:8). We must also depend on Him to accomplish the mission of God through us. Finally, we must believe that just as He powerfully used the early church to advance the *missio Dei*, He will powerfully use us today.

A People of the Word

Not only will a true people of the Spirit be a missionary people, but they will also be a people of the Word. Because of their experience with God's missionary Spirit, God's missionary people will be committed to God's missionary book, the Bible.

Earlier in this chapter, we discussed how the Bible itself is a product of the missionary work of the Holy Spirit. God's missionary Spirit inspired the Holy Scriptures so that humans could come to know God and do His will. The Scriptures are God's unchanging revelation of himself and His will to humanity. Through His Spirit and His Word, God is at work calling, saving, and sanctifying a people for himself through faith in Christ. Now, because God's Spirit dwells within us, we should be a people of the Word. We should depend on the Bible as our source of truth and our guide for faith and practice. Further, as we diligently study the Bible, we should expect the Holy Spirit to help us understand its message.

Finally, we must commit ourselves to proclaiming God's Word to all people. In faith and with boldness we must call a lost world to repentance and faith in Christ. As we do this, we should expect the missionary Spirit to anoint our words through His power. We should realize that every Spirit-anointed proclamation of the Word is a continuation of the missionary activity the Spirit began when He inspired the Bible.

Chapter 3 – The Holy Spirit: A Missionary Spirit

Questions for Discussion and Reflection

1. Do you think it is accurate to call the Holy Spirit a missionary Spirit? Explain your answer.

2. In what ways might a missiological reading of the Bible affect you and your church?

3. In addition to the Bible's own claim of inspiration by the Holy Spirit, can you think of any other evidence that support the idea that the Spirit of God is the divine author of Scripture?

4. How would you explain the difference between the theological concepts of revelation, inspiration, and illumination to a new follower of Christ?

5. How might the concepts of revelation, inspiration and illumination affect the way we study the Bible and prepare to preach and teach from it?

6. How important is the Bible in testing claims about theology, prophecy, and the operation of the gifts of the Spirit? Is it possible the Holy Spirit would ever give us directions that are contrary to clear teachings in Scripture?

Chapter 3 – The Holy Spirit: A Missionary Spirit

~ Part Two ~

The Missionary Spirit in the Old Testament

~ CHAPTER 4 ~

THE MISSIONARY SPIRIT PREPARES GOD'S PEOPLE

THE MISSIONARY SPIRIT PREPARES A PEOPLE FOR GOD

This chapter and the next will examine the work of the Spirit in the Old Testament. The Old Testament is an important source of information about the Holy Spirit, and there is much we can learn from it concerning His work. As we examine the Old Testament, we will see how the Holy Spirit was actively working to accomplish the mission of God to prepare a people for himself.

The Spirit Participated in God's Mission at Creation

The first verses of the Bible describe how God created the heavens and the earth. From the beginning, the Spirit of God was actively participating. Genesis 1:2 states that the Spirit (Hebrew: *Ruach*) of God was hovering over the water that covered the earth.

Then we read how God repeatedly spoke different things into existence (Genesis 1:3, 6, 9, 11, 14, 20, 24). The close connection of the presence of the Spirit and God's speaking seems to imply that God spoke by His Spirit to bring creation into being. The psalmist made this connection when he declared, "By the word of the LORD the heavens were made, their starry host by the breath [*Ruach*] of his mouth" (Psalm 33:6). The parallel style of Hebrew poetry in this verse supports the idea that God spoke by the (*Ruach*) Spirit when He created the world. Psalm 104:30 also affirms that the Spirit of God participated in the work of creation.

The creation of humankind is the ultimate purpose of the creation story. After God formed the first man, He "breathed into his nostrils the breath of life, and the man became a living being" (Genesis 2:7). In a number of Scriptures, the phrase "breath of God" is a metaphor used to describe the Spirit of God creating and giving life (Job 27:3; 32:8; 34:14–15; Isaiah 42:5).

We can conclude that the Holy Spirit was a full participant with the Father (Genesis 1:1) and Son (John 1:1–3) in the creation of the world and humankind. Horton explains: "The Bible ascribes all the works of God in an absolute sense to each member of the Trinity both individually and collectively. Each of the divine Persons has His specific function. Yet they all work in perfect harmony and cooperation at all times."[11] This is important to keep in mind. Our study of pneumatology is intended to highlight and help us appreciate the work of the Spirit. However, the Holy Spirit does not act independently of the other members of the Trinity. Throughout this study we are emphasizing that the work of the Spirit is correctly understood in the context of the mission of God. The work of the Spirit in the creation of humankind shows that from the beginning,

---

[11] Stanley M. Horton, *What the Bible Says About the Holy Spirit*, rev. ed. (Springfield, MO: Gospel Publishing House, 2005), 17.

The Spirit Continued to Work in Humankind After the Fall

Genesis 3 describes the sad story of the fall of humankind into sin. Adam and Eve's disobedience disrupted God's plan to create a world of people living in relationship with Him. Nevertheless, God continued to work by His Spirit to restrain sin and to draw people back into relationship with Him. Later in this study, when we examine the work of the Spirit in the New Testament, we will discover that one important work of the Spirit in God's mission is to convict people of sin and draw them back to God (John 16:7–11).

Over time, the people's rebellion became so great that God "regretted that he had made human beings on the earth, and his heart was deeply troubled" (Genesis 6:5–6). As a result, He said, "My Spirit will not contend with humans forever, for they are mortal [or flesh]" (6:3). Flattery notes how this verse makes a contrast between "Spirit" and "flesh." This implies that humankind is influenced by the sinful nature as well as by the Spirit of God.[12] If people resist God enough, there comes a point at which He will stop drawing them by His Spirit. The apostle Paul describes this in Romans 1:18–25: "God gave them over in the sinful desires of their hearts" to immorality (1:24).

As a result of this rebellion, God decided to judge the world by destroying humankind through a flood (Genesis 6:7). Noah, however, was the one person on earth who pleased God. Therefore, God spared Noah and his family, and through him God began again His work of creating a righteous people for himself. Later, God chose Abraham and began working through him and his descendants to accomplish His mission.

---

[12] George M. Flattery, *A Biblical Theology of the Holy Spirit: Old Testament* (Springfield, MO: Global University, 2009), 37.

Chapter 4 ~ The Missionary Spirit Prepares God's People

The Spirit Worked to Form Israel as a Nation Dedicated to God and His Mission

The Spirit Worked in the Patriarchs to Begin Forming God's People

God called Abraham and promised to bless him and to bless the entire world through him (Genesis 12:1–3). God did this to advance His plan to form a people who would serve Him and through whom He could work to accomplish His mission of bringing all nations into the blessing of life and relationship with Him (Genesis 12:3; Galatians 3:8–9). He would mediate this blessing to the nations through the Holy Spirit (Galatians 3:14).

The Holy Spirit worked in the formation of Israel through the patriarchs. We know this because the Old Testament refers to each of these men as "prophets" and "anointed ones":

- Abraham (Genesis 20:7; Psalm 105:9, 15; see also 1 Chronicles 16:16, 22)
- Isaac (Psalm 105:9, 15; see also 1 Chronicles 16:16, 22)
- Jacob (Psalm 105:10, 15; see also 1 Chronicles 16:17, 22)

An Old Testament prophet was someone who was anointed by God and who "spoke from God as they were carried along by the Holy Spirit" (2 Peter 1:21). Genesis tells how God spoke to these three men, revealing himself to them in dreams and visions just as He did with other Old Testament prophets. Because we know that they were anointed prophets, we also know that the Holy Spirit was working through them to accomplish His work.

This work of the Spirit continued in Jacob's son Joseph. At times, God revealed himself to Joseph in dreams (Genesis 37:5–10). He also gave Joseph the ability to interpret other people's dreams (40:5–22; 41:9–36). Pharaoh acknowledged this ability to be a work of the

"Spirit of God" (41:38). Through Joseph's Spirit-empowered service, God preserved Joseph's family during a great famine and caused them to move to Egypt where they multiplied and became the great nation God had promised to Abraham.

The Spirit Worked in Liberating Israel so the Nation Could Serve God and His Mission

After many years in Egypt, the Israelites grew into a great nation. During that time, they became slaves to the Egyptians. However, God intervened, setting them free and taking them back to Canaan, the land He had first promised to Abraham. The Holy Spirit played a significant role in this important part of God's mission.

In Chapter 2 we discovered how in Scripture, the hand or arm of God is often used to symbolize God's Spirit. In fact, in Exodus, Numbers, and Deuteronomy, this symbol is used at least thirty-three times.[13] Each time, it refers to the powerful miracles God performed to liberate the nation of Israel from Egyptian bondage and bring them into the Promised Land.

In Deuteronomy 4 the writer connected God's "mighty hand" and "outstretched arm" (4:34) with His divine "Presence" (4:37). However, Isaiah 63 contains what could be the clearest connection between the arm of God and the Holy Spirit in liberating Israel. In that passage, the prophet told us that even though the Israelites were disobedient and "grieved his Holy Spirit," God placed His Spirit among them in the days of Moses (Isaiah 63:10–11). Isaiah then described how God worked by "his glorious arm of power" to liberate Israel (63:12). The prophet concluded that God gave His people "rest by the Spirit of the LORD," and by doing this He "guided [His] people to make for [himself] a glorious name" (63:14). This and other

---

[13] Ex. 3:19; 3:20; 6:6; 7:5; 8:19; 9:3; 9:15; 13:3; 13:9; 13:14; 13:16; 15:6; 15:12; 15:16; 32:11. Num. 11:23. Deut. 2:15; 3:24; 4:34; 5:15; 6:21; 7:8; 7:19; 9:26; 9:29; 11:2; 26:8

passages clearly demonstrate that the hand or arm of the Lord was indeed the Holy Spirit acting to advance God's mission (1 Chronicles 28:12,19; Ezekiel 3:14).

Today the Spirit of God continues to work in the mission of setting people free. He sets them free from slavery to sin and Satan (Galatians 4:4–7). When people accept Christ as Lord of their lives, the Holy Spirit transforms them from slaves into children of God (John 3:6–8; Romans 8:14–16).

The Spirit of God Dwelt with Israel in the Tabernacle

After God liberated Israel from slavery, He told Moses to have the people "make a sanctuary for me, and I will dwell among them" (Exodus 25:8). He later added that this sanctuary was to be dedicated to serve as His dwelling place among the people (29:45-46). This is the very reason He brought them out of Egypt—so that He could dwell among them and be their God. When Moses finished placing the furnishings inside the tabernacle, the cloud that had guided Israel from Egypt to Mount Sinai covered the tabernacle, and the place was filled with the glory of the Lord (Exodus 40:34–35). This dramatic scene demonstrated that the Spirit of God was present and dwelling among His people. Years later, a similar thing occurred when Solomon finished building the temple in Jerusalem. Again a cloud and the glory of God filled the temple, demonstrating that God's Spirit was present (1 Kings 8:10–11).

Building the tabernacle in the desert was an important part of God's mission. The theme of God dwelling with His people is a frequently repeated theme throughout Scripture. Later in this study we will see how the church and individual believers become God's temple and serve as the dwelling place of God's Spirit (1 Corinthians 3:16; 6:19; 2 Corinthians 6:16). The book of Revelation gives us a glimpse of God's ultimate purpose. It declares that when God has completed His mission of redeeming people from every nation

(Revelation 5:9–10), He will make His permanent dwelling with humankind. "He will dwell with them. They will be his people, and God himself will be with them and be their God" (21:3).

The Spirit Dwelt with Israel to Help Them Serve God's Mission

God chose Israel to serve Him, and He placed His Holy Spirit among them for a purpose. In Exodus 19, God declared His missionary purpose for the nation of Israel. He said to the people: "If you obey me fully and keep my covenant, then out of all nations you will be my treasured possession. Although the whole earth is mine, you will be for me a kingdom of priests and a holy nation" (19:5–6). In effect, God called the whole nation to act in a priestly role to the rest of the world. The whole earth belongs to God, and His desire is to dwell with people from all nations.

God chose Israel and placed His Holy Spirit among them so that they might become a missionary people. He does the same today; He has placed His Spirit in His church that we might be His witnesses to the ends of the earth (Acts 1:8). Since it is God's mission to save the nations, we will now begin to look at how God worked by His Spirit to enable His Old Testament people to participate in that mission.

THE MISSIONARY SPIRIT EMPOWERS GOD'S PEOPLE FOR MISSION

Anthony Palma has rightly stated that "spiritual tasks can be accomplished only by the enabling power of the Holy Spirit."[14] The Old Testament repeatedly testifies to this fact. God delivered Israel from Egyptian slavery and gave them a mission to serve Him and represent Him to the nations of the world. He dwelt among them through His presence in the tabernacle. However, they needed more

---

[14] Palma, *The Holy Spirit*, 37.

than that. They needed the Spirit's enabling power to come on them to enable them to accomplish God's work.

One major theme of the Spirit's work in the Old Testament is that He came on the leaders and enabled them to lead Israel to serve God and His mission. These leaders included prophets, judges, and kings. The Spirit empowered others to work as artisans and builders. God called each one to serve and take part in His purpose and mission. We will now look at some of these individuals. Each one demonstrates that the work of God is accomplished not by human striving but by people empowered by God's Spirit (Zechariah 4:6).

The Spirit Empowered Moses, Joshua, and Seventy Elders

Moses was the first great Spirit-empowered leader of Israel. God worked through him with powerful signs and wonders to liberate Israel from slavery and to form them into a great nation with laws and government. Significantly, the Spirit also enabled Moses to write the first five books of the Bible.

What made Moses a capable leader? The Holy Spirit empowered him for leadership. Numbers 11:1–17 contains an important story regarding the need for leaders and all of God's people to be empowered by the Spirit.

Moses was overwhelmed by the burden of leading the nation, so he prayed to God, asking Him for help (Numbers 11:11–15). God responded by showing Moses that the answer to his dilemma was the multiplication of Spirit-empowered leaders. God told Moses to gather seventy elders of the people and bring them to the tabernacle. He said to Moses, "I will take some of the power of the Spirit that is on you and put it on them. They will share the burden of the people with you so that you will not have to carry it alone" (11:17). God did not want His people to be dependent on one Spirit-anointed leader, so He provided for them by raising up many leaders who were empowered by the Spirit. The same is true today.

Chapter 4 ~ The Missionary Spirit Prepares God's People

There is more we can learn from this story. We learn how God fulfilled His promise to put His Spirit on the seventy elders. He gave them a sign that the Spirit had come on them—they began to prophesy (Numbers 11:25). The same is true today. When God pours out His Spirit on His children, He enables them to speak Spirit-inspired words (Acts 2:4; 10:46; 19:6). When Joshua saw two of the men prophesying in the camp, he was disturbed, for they had not obeyed Moses' order to come to the tabernacle. He urged Moses to stop them. Moses answered Joshua, "Are you jealous for my sake? I wish that all the LORD's people were prophets and that the LORD would put his Spirit on them" (Numbers 11:29). Moses recognized that the Spirit of God had made the difference in his own life and service, and he wanted all of God's peoples to experience the same presence and power of the Spirit. Years later, Joel prophesied of a time when God would pour out His Spirit on all of His people (Joel 2:28–29). At Pentecost, Peter announced that the promise had been fulfilled (Acts 2:17–18). Today, all of God's children can experience the presence and power of God in their lives and ministries (2:38–39). What Moses longed for is not only possible, but it is what God will do for His church if we will believe and ask Him to pour out His Spirit on us.

God continued to choose leaders and empower them by His Spirit to lead His people. For instance, God chose Joshua to succeed Moses as the leader of Israel. He told Moses that Joshua was the right person to be the next leader because the Spirit was in him (Numbers 27:18). According to Flattery: "The story of Joshua once again demonstrates the importance of the Spirit's presence to authenticate and empower the leaders of Israel. The specific responsibilities vary, but the empowerment is the constant need."[15] All of God's people need that same empowerment today.

---

[15] Flattery, *A Biblical Theology of the Holy Spirit: Old Testament*, 60.

The Spirit Empowered Artisans to Build God's House

Another Old Testament example of those who were filled with the Spirit and enabled to do the work of God are two men named Bezalel and Oholiab. They helped in the construction of the tabernacle in the wilderness. These men were "filled...with the Spirit of God, with wisdom, with understanding, with knowledge and with all kinds of skills—to make artistic designs for work in gold, silver and bronze, to cut and set stones, to work in wood, and to engage in all kinds of crafts" (Exodus 31:3–5). We need many practical skills to accomplish God's mission on earth, and He is ready to supply such abilities to His people by His Spirit.

The Spirit Empowered Judges to Deliver God's People

The book of Judges tells the history of Israel after the death of Joshua up until the time of Saul, the first king of Israel. During this era, God's people often found themselves in great trouble because of their sin and unfaithfulness to God (Judges 2:11–23). However, when they repented and cried out to God, He raised up leaders called "judges" whom He empowered by His Spirit to deliver Israel. The Holy Spirit would come on them to give them supernatural ability to fight and deliver Israel from their oppressors. Here is what the book of Judges says about the Holy Spirit empowering these individuals:

- Othniel: "The Spirit of the LORD came on him" (3:10).
- Gideon: "Then the Spirit of the LORD came on Gideon" (6:34).
- Jepthah: "Then the Spirit of the LORD came on Jephthah" (11:29).
- Samson: "And the Spirit of the LORD began to stir him" (13:25); "The Spirit of the LORD came powerfully upon him" (14:6, 19; 15:14).

The enabling power of the Holy Spirit was the key to the ability of these leaders.

The Spirit Empowered Kings to Lead God's People

Israel's first two kings, Saul and David, were both empowered by the Holy Spirit to lead the nation. The prophet Samuel anointed both with oil (1 Samuel 10:1; 16:13). This anointing oil was symbolic of God's choice of these men as leaders in Israel. Even more, it was symbolic of the anointing of the Holy Spirit on them to empower them to lead God's people.

When Samuel anointed Saul to be king, the Spirit of God came on the king changing him into a different man and enabling him to prophesy (1 Samuel 10:1–10). The presence and the power of the Spirit then enabled the king to lead Israel courageously in battle against its enemies (11:5–11). Sadly, however, the story shows that even though the Spirit gave Saul courage and the ability to lead, Saul did not commit his heart to obey the Lord faithfully. Because of his repeated acts of disobedience, God removed His Spirit from Saul and chose David to take his place as king over Israel (15:10; 16:1–14). Saul's example demonstrates how important it is for an anointed servant of God to humbly and continually seek God and to walk in obedience to His Word. God gives His anointing to His servants, but He will take it away if they do not serve Him from their hearts.

When Samuel anointed David as king, the Holy Spirit came powerfully upon him just as He had come on Saul (1 Samuel 16:13). In contrast to Saul, David served God faithfully throughout his life. David's life was not perfect, and he later committed a terrible sin against God (2 Samuel 11). Yet unlike Saul, David repented and sought God's forgiveness. David's prayer in Psalm 51 is a powerful model of repentance. He cried out to God asking for forgiveness, and he asked God not to take His Holy Spirit from him (Psalm 51:11). In this Psalm, David promised that if God would answer his prayer, he would proclaim God's word to others. The result would be the salvation of sinners (51:13). David recognized that, as a Spirit-empowered leader, he was responsible to proclaim the word of God and to lead people to faith in God.

God answered David's prayer and forgave him. As a result, the Holy Spirit continued to work in David until the end of his life. In his last words David declared, "The Spirit of the LORD spoke through me; his word was on my tongue" (2 Samuel 23:2). The presence and power of the Holy Spirit was the key to David's effective leadership of God's people and mission, and it is the key to effective spiritual leadership today.

After David, the Old Testament does not describe any other king as being empowered by the Spirit. Solomon received the gift of great wisdom from God, which undoubtedly came from the Holy Spirit. However, Solomon and most of the kings who followed him failed to serve God fully as David had done. Throughout the rest of the period of the kings, the exile, and return from Babylon, the Old Testament emphasizes the work of the Spirit through another type of leader—the prophets.

The Spirit Empowered Prophets to Proclaim God's Word

The largest group of Spirit-empowered leaders in the Old Testament was the prophets. They were men and women of the Spirit. The anointing and power of the Holy Spirit on these individuals qualified and enabled them to perform their essential roles as spokespersons for God (2 Peter 1:21).

Definition of Prophecy

Spirit-inspired prophecy is an important Old Testament topic. In the Old Testament, the most common result of the Spirit coming on people was that they spoke Spirit-inspired words; that is, they prophesied. Stanley Horton notes, "The entire Old Testament looks on prophecy as the chief activity of the Spirit among His people."[16] It is therefore important to understand the meaning of the term *prophecy* as it is used in the Old Testament.

Generally, prophecy means an "inspired utterance." Genuine prophecies were messages given by men or women of God as they were moved by the Holy Spirit. Sometimes these messages were predictions of future events. For instance, many were predictions concerning the coming Messiah who would establish the kingdom of God. In most of the prophecies, however, the Holy Spirit inspired the prophets to speak messages to the people concerning their current situation and relationship with God.

Prophets Called People to Repent and Represent God to the Nations

The prophets were inspired by the Holy Spirit primarily to call people to repentance and to a renewed commitment to serve God and remain true to His mission. Second Chronicles 24:19 says, "Although the LORD sent prophets to the people to bring them back to him, and though they testified against them, they would not listen" (see also 2 Kings 17:13–14; Jeremiah 7:25–26; 35:15). Isaiah wrote how the people's rebellion and sin grieved the Holy Spirit (Isaiah 63:10).

God had called and chosen Israel to participate in His mission to save the nations. Therefore, the repeated cycles of rebellion and sin throughout Israel's history not only affected their personal relationship with God, but it also affected their testimony to the rest of the world. The Holy Spirit inspired the prophet Ezekiel to speak repeatedly about the way the nation of Israel had profaned the name of the Lord among the nations (see also Ezekiel 20:1–44; 36:16–23; 39:7).

God's mission to save the nations was an essential part of the work of the Spirit through the Old Testament prophets. When God

---

[16] Horton, *What the Bible Says About the Holy Spirit*, 55.

called Jeremiah, He told him, "Before you were born I set you apart; I appointed you as a prophet to the nations" (Jeremiah 1:5). God even sent the prophet Jonah to warn the city of Nineveh of coming judgment. The work of the prophets to call Israel back to obedience to God was connected to God's mission for the nation of Israel.

False Prophets

The Old Testament also contains strong warnings against people who present themselves as prophets of God but who do not proclaim God's word by the power of His Spirit (see also Jeremiah 14:13–15; Ezekiel 13:1–9; and Micah 3:5–7, 11). There were many who falsely prophesied peace, blessing, and prosperity in the name of the Lord rather than call people to repentance and commitment to God. Their prophecies were not inspired by the Spirit; they were inspired by personal greed.

The Old Testament gives a harsh condemnation against such false prophets who pretend to speak by the inspiration of the Spirit. God warned His people not to listen to them. Moses warned that even if the prophet performed a sign or wonder, the people should not listen to that prophet if his message drew people away from obedience to God's word (Deuteronomy 13:1–4). Prophetic messages and even miracles are not in themselves proof that someone is a genuine prophet sent and anointed by the Spirit of God. The prophet's message must conform to the sound doctrine found in all of Scripture and must lead people to obey God and to support His mission to save the lost.

This is an important and relevant truth for us today. There continue to be false prophets who proclaim blessing and prosperity but who do not lead people to repentance and commitment to Christ and His mission. Jesus warned that "false messiahs and false prophets will appear and perform signs and wonders to deceive, if possible, the elect" (Mark 13:22). Therefore, He warned that we should be on our guard. Miracles are a sign of a prophet of God, but they are not the only sign. Jesus also explained that the spiritual fruit or evidence in a person's life must demonstrate that they do the will of the Father (Matthew 7:15–23).

The Spirit Continually Worked to Accomplish God's Mission Through His People

The story of Israel in the Old Testament reveals that, rather than faithfully serve God and His mission, the nation often chose to rebel against Him. The Spirit of God repeatedly warned Israel through the prophets that if they did not repent, they would suffer God's judgment. Eventually God allowed foreign nations to conquer Israel and take them into captivity. Nevertheless, even though God's people failed Him, He did not stop working to accomplish His mission through them.

After seventy years of exile, God made it possible for a remnant of Israelites to return to Jerusalem and rebuild the city and the temple. The prophets Haggai and Zechariah encouraged the people that even though they were weak and small in number, they would succeed because God's Holy Spirit was present and working to enable them (Haggai 2:4–5; Zechariah 4:6). These passages show that the Spirit was still working to accomplish God's mission through His people. They also show that God chooses to work through weak vessels to accomplish His mission by the power of His Spirit. This truth should encourage us that, if we will seek to be filled with His Spirit, God will use us to accomplish His work even when we are weak and feel unable.

KEY TERMS RELATED TO EMPOWERMENT AND THE WORK OF THE SPIRIT IN THE OLD TESTAMENT

The Old Testament uses several words and phrases to describe how the Spirit empowers people to serve. As you read the Old

Testament, take note of these terms. The New Testament also uses many of these words and phrases in relation to the work of the Spirit. This is especially true in the books of Luke and Acts.

The Spirit "comes on"

The phrase "come on," and similar terms, are possibly the most commonly used terms in the Old Testament to describe the Spirit's work of empowering and inspiring God's servants:

- He *comes on* (Numbers 24:2; Judges 3:10; 6:34; 11:29; 1 Samuel 19:20, 23; 1 Chronicles 12:18; 2 Chronicles 15:1; 24:20; Isaiah 42:1; 61:1).
- He *comes powerfully upon* (Judges 14:6, 19; 15:14; 1 Samuel 10:6, 10; 11:6; 16:13).
- He *rests upon* (Numbers 11:25–26; 2 Kings 2:15; Isaiah 11:2).
- He is *poured out* (Isaiah 32:15; Ezekiel 39:29; Joel 2:28–29).
- He is *given* (Nehemiah 9:20).

The Spirit "fills" and is "in"

The Old Testament also uses the words *fill* and *in* to describe how the Spirit empowers and inspires God's servants:

- He *fills* (Exodus 31:3; 35:31; Deuteronomy 34:9; Micah 3:8).
- He is *in* (Genesis 41:38; Numbers 27:18; Ezekiel 2:2; 3:24; 36:26; Daniel 4:8–9; 5:11, 14).

The Spirit "speaks"

- The Spirit is also said to *speak* to and through His prophets (2 Samuel 23:2; Ezekiel 3:24; 11:5).

Chapter 4 ~ The Missionary Spirit Prepares God's People

IMPLICATIONS AND APPLICATIONS

In this chapter, we have seen that throughout the Old Testament, the Holy Spirit actively participated in God's mission. The Spirit's participation in creation shows that He was involved in carrying out God's mission from the beginning of time. This insight inspires us to pay careful attention to the work of the Spirit throughout the rest of Scripture. When we see the Spirit at work in each stage of the development of God's mission, we come to realize that our participation in any part of God's work requires us to be people of the Spirit.

When we read how God repeatedly gave His Spirit to the leaders of Israel, we realize the importance of choosing leaders who are full of the Spirit and empowered by Him to do God's work. The church today should put no less emphasis on leaders being filled with the Spirit. God is ready to empower His people for every task needed to accomplish His mission. However, leaders must be continually filled with the presence and power of the Spirit. Sometimes, due to the need for workers, church leaders are tempted to appoint people who have not been filled with the Spirit. This is a serious mistake and should be avoided. God's answer is for leaders to seek His help and endeavor to see more people filled with the Spirit. The Spirit alone can enable people to serve the way God intends them to serve.

The stories of Saul and David show us that the presence of the Holy Spirit in one's life is a valuable gift from God and that it can be lost through willful disobedience. No one should take the anointing of the Holy Spirit for granted. We must each walk humbly before God in faithful obedience to His Word and His will. Further, we must nurture the anointing of the Holy Spirit on our lives through prayer, humility, and repentance.

The powerful role of the Old Testament prophets reminds us how much God's people need leaders who are full of the Spirit and who will speak God's Word in the power and anointing of the Holy Spirit.

This will help God's people remain committed to Him and obedient to His mission. It is unfortunate, however, that so many Pentecostal leaders have fallen into the temptation of using prophetic ministry and miracles to attract people to themselves and for personal financial gain. Men and women of God must guard against the temptation to manipulate the power of the Spirit. The example of the Old Testament false prophets warns us how wrong it is to misuse prophecy and spiritual power for personal gain. God's people need true prophets who serve Him with humility and sincerity and who help God's people build the kingdom of God.

Today, just as in the time of Zechariah and Haggai, God promises to empower His people by His Spirit. When God's people feel weak and discouraged, the Spirit of God is ready to work powerfully through them to accomplish God's mission. We must never stop depending on and seeking the power of the Spirit. God loves to work powerfully through those who are weak in the eyes of the world.

Chapter 4 ~ The Missionary Spirit Prepares God's People

Questions for Discussion and Reflection

1. What are some similarities and differences between the way the Holy Spirit worked in God's people in the Old Testament compared to the way He works in the church today?

2. Is it ever acceptable to appoint leaders in the church who have not been filled with the Holy Spirit?

3. What action should we take when there are people in the church who have not been filled with the Spirit?

4. Many leaders in the church today use the title "prophet." How should the church respond, and how can we determine if someone is truly a prophet today?

Chapter 4 ~ The Missionary Spirit Prepares God's People

~ CHAPTER 5 ~

THE MISSIONARY SPIRIT REVEALS GOD'S MISSION

THE FUTURE AGE OF THE SPIRIT

In Chapter 4, we learned how the Holy Spirit was active throughout the Old Testament, preparing a people for God and enabling leaders. Not only was the Spirit present among them, He also worked in and through them in powerful ways. At certain times, He empowered leaders and prophets to speak for Him and to perform tasks to advance His mission.

Moses, however, longed for a day when God would put His Spirit on all His people, enabling them to speak prophetically on His behalf (Numbers 11:29). Years later, the prophet Joel announced that this was indeed God's plan. One day, God would pour out His Spirit on all His people (Joel 2:28–29). In this chapter, we will examine Old Testament prophecies that foretold a time when a Spirit-anointed descendant of King David would come to establish God's eternal kingdom. It would be a time when God would pour out His Spirit on all His people, transforming them and empowering them for His mission.

THE SPIRIT WILL EMPOWER THE MESSIAH FOR GOD'S MISSION

God's Promise of an Anointed King

Nearly a thousand years before the birth of Christ, God promised King David: "I will raise up your offspring to succeed you, one of your own sons, and I will establish his kingdom.... I will set him over my house and my kingdom forever; his throne will be established forever" (1 Chronicles 17:11, 14). This announcement marks an important step in the fulfillment of God's mission. We have already discussed how God chose Abraham and promised to bless all nations through him and his descendants (Genesis 12:3; 22:18). Now, in this promise to David, God revealed more details about how He was going to bless the nations. He would do this by establishing an eternal kingdom, and a descendant of David would rule on its throne forever.

When the angel Gabriel announced to the virgin Mary that she was going to bear a son, he told her: "He will be great and will be called the Son of the Most High. The Lord God will give him the throne of his father David, and he will reign over Jacob's descendants forever; his kingdom will never end" (Luke 1:32–33). Jesus would fulfill the promises that God made to Abraham and David (Matthew 1:1; Galatians 3:8, 16). Through Christ, God opened the door for all people to be reconciled to Him and to enter His eternal kingdom.

The Old Testament further reveals that the Holy Spirit would play a key role in the fulfillment of these promises. Following God's promise to King David, the prophets often reminded the people that God was going to raise up a son of David who would establish an eternal kingdom. The prophets also revealed that this future Davidic king would be anointed by the Holy Spirit. The Holy Spirit would enable him to accomplish the mission of establishing God's eternal kingdom. Just as King David was anointed and empowered by the Holy Spirit to lead Israel, this future king would also be anointed and empowered by the Spirit.

The Meaning of the Terms "Messiah" and "Christ"

In the church, Jesus is often called the Messiah. The word *Messiah* is a transliteration of a Hebrew word *mashiah,* which means "anointed." The Old Testament kings of Israel were sometimes referred to as "the Lord's anointed" (1 Samuel 16:6, 13; 24:10; 2 Chronicles 6:42; Psalm 2:2). It should be no surprise, then, that many of the Old Testament prophecies concerning the future son of David include the idea of his being "anointed." For instance, Daniel prophesied, "The Anointed One will be put to death and will have nothing" (Daniel 9:26). Some Bible translations use the word "Messiah" instead of "Anointed One" in verses 25 and 26.

Interestingly, the word for *Messiah* appears only twice in the Greek New Testament (John 1:41; 4:25). However, the word *Christ,* which is a transliteration of the Greek word *Christus,* also meaning "anointed," is used more than 500 times to refer to Jesus. These titles—Messiah and Christ—point to the fact that God anointed Jesus with the Holy Spirit to enable Him to accomplish the mission for which He was sent.

Prophecies of the Spirit's Power on the Messiah

The Old Testament contains a number of prophecies concerning the power of the Spirit that would rest on the Messiah enabling him to establish God's kingdom. Let us look at some of those prophecies.

The Spirit and the Branch

The book of Isaiah was written about 700 years before the birth of Christ. It contains many prophecies concerning the Messiah. Several of these describe how He would be anointed and empowered by the Spirit. The prophecies in Isaiah also identify the messiah as a descendant of David who would rule over God's kingdom. For example, in one passage Isaiah predicted that the family of Jesse, King David's father, would become like a tree that had been cut down with only its stump remaining in the ground (11:1). This prophecy was fulfilled when the Babylonians conquered Judah in 586 B.C. Since that time, a descendant of David has never ruled as king over the political nation of Israel.

However, this was not the end of Isaiah's prophecy. He also declared that one day a shoot would come out of that stump and become a branch that bears fruit (Isaiah 11:1). Isaiah used this picture to show that a future descendant of David would come, and this descendant would once again take the place as king over God's people.

Then Isaiah declared, "The Spirit of the LORD will rest on him—the Spirit of wisdom and of understanding, the Spirit of counsel and of might, the Spirit of knowledge and fear of the LORD" (Isaiah 11:2). In other words, the Holy Spirit would rest on this future king in a powerful way and give him the ability to rule. We can divide these Spirit-given abilities into three groups.

First, the king would have the "Spirit of wisdom and understanding." These abilities would enable him to make right and just decisions (see also Isaiah 11:3–4). Second, the king would have the "Spirit of counsel and of might." These abilities would enable him to destroy God's enemies and bring peace to the earth. Isaiah describes in verses 4–9 how this would be accomplished. Third, the king would be given the "Spirit of knowledge and fear of the LORD." These abilities would enable him to be spiritual leader for the entire world. As a result, "the earth will be filled with the knowledge of the LORD" (11:9).

The remainder of Isaiah 11 describes how this Spirit-empowered descendant of David would establish the kingdom of God. His kingdom would include more than just the nation of Israel, for "in that day the Root of Jesse will stand as a banner for the peoples; the nations will rally to him" (11:10). The coming messianic king would thus be empowered by the Spirit for the mission of God, and His reign over the kingdom of God would bring God's blessing to all nations.

The Spirit and the Servant of the Lord

Another image Isaiah often used to refer to the Messiah is the image of the "Servant of the Lord." Sometimes Isaiah used the term to refer to the nation of Israel. Primarily, however, he used the term to speak of the Messiah who would come to establish God's kingdom and accomplish His mission of saving the nations. Isaiah graphically described how this Servant of the Lord would suffer and die for the sins of the world (52:13–53:12). He wrote, "The LORD has laid on him the iniquity of us all" (53:6). Such a sacrifice was necessary because sin is the core problem that separates people from God (59:1–2). Isaiah 53:1–7 is a powerful description of how Jesus suffered on the cross to redeem people from sin.

To accomplish His messianic mission, the Servant of the Lord would need to be empowered by the Holy Spirit. Through Isaiah, God said of Him, "Here is my servant, whom I uphold, my chosen one in whom I delight; I will put my Spirit on him, and he will bring justice to the nations" (Isaiah 42:1). Isaiah thus connects the power of the Spirit resting on the Messiah with His redemptive work. In his gospel, Matthew reveals that Jesus' Spirit-empowered healing ministry was a fulfillment of this prophecy (Matthew 12:18–21; see also Acts 10:38). Isaiah goes on to say of the Messiah that "in his teaching the islands will put their hope" (42:4). Some identify these islands as distant lands or foreign nations. As a result, the Messiah will be "a light for the Gentiles" (42:6), and He will bring "salvation…to the ends of the earth" (49:6).

Isaiah 61:1–2 is another important passage that describes how the Servant of the Lord would be empowered by the Holy Spirit. More than 700 years later, Jesus announced that He was fulfilling this prophecy (Luke 4:16-21). Find this passage in your Bible and read it now. Notice how this prophecy emphasizes that the Messiah would be anointed and empowered by the Spirit. The purpose of the Spirit's power on Him was to enable Him to fulfill the mission that God had given Him, that is, the mission of proclaiming the gospel and setting captives free.

These prophecies are important because they help us understand how God intended to advance His mission through the ministry of Jesus Christ, who would be wholly dependent on the power of the Holy Spirit. While the Spirit had empowered previous kings of Israel to lead the nation of Israel, God was planning to put His Spirit on this King in a unique and powerful way; He would be empowered to bring salvation to the entire world. The Spirit would rest on Him "without limit" (John 3:34).

Prophecies of the Spirit on the Messiah's People

In Isaiah 53, the prophet spoke of the Messiah suffering and dying for the sins of all people (53:4–7). He then declared that God would "prolong his days" (53:10). These prophecies pointed to the death and resurrection of Jesus. In that same chapter, Isaiah spoke of the Messiah's "offspring," or spiritual children (53:10). These are people who would one day be born into His kingdom by putting their faith in Him. They are the church of Jesus Christ of which we are now a part.

Two other passages in Isaiah describe how the Messiah's children, like the Messiah himself, would receive the empowering gift of the Holy Spirit. In Isaiah 44:3, God promised the Messiah, "I will pour out my Spirit on your offspring." Then in chapter 59, Isaiah again quoted God as saying to the coming Redeemer, "My Spirit, who is on you, will not depart from you, and my words that I have put in your mouth will always be on your lips and on the lips of your children and on the lips of their descendants—from this time on and forever" (59:21).

The gift of the Spirit, which would rest on the Messiah and enable Him to fulfill God's mission, was also promised to the Messiah's descendants, and the Spirit will remain with them forever. Jesus made a similar promise to His disciples: "I will ask the Father, and He will give you another Helper, that He may be with you forever; that is the Spirit of truth" (John 14:16–17, NASB).

Additionally, the Holy Spirit would inspire the Messiah's words, for God would put His words in the Messiah's mouth (Isaiah 59:21). In a similar way, the Spirit would be on the Messiah's offspring, filling their mouths with the word of the Lord. We will discuss this powerful truth in more detail when we look at the work of the Spirit to empower the Messiah's people for God's mission.

Summary

The prophets spoke of a future work that God intended to do by His Spirit. This work would be connected to God's mission of creating a people for himself from all nations. Isaiah revealed that a powerful, Spirit-anointed descendant of David would carry out the mission. This Son of David would establish an eternal and perfect kingdom. In the Spirit's power, He would announce the good news of the kingdom and offer himself as a sacrifice to redeem humankind. God further revealed that He planned to give His Spirit to all those who repented of their sins and turned to follow His anointed King. This gift of the Spirit would be for people of all nations.

Now we will look at other prophecies concerning the future work of the Holy Spirit in the lives of those who would repent and follow the Messiah. The prophets spoke about a work of the Spirit to transform the hearts and lives of people. They also foretold a time when God's people would be empowered by the Spirit to participate in God's mission.

THE SPIRIT WILL ENABLE THE MESSIAH'S PEOPLE TO LIVE FOR GOD

From beginning to end, the Old Testament tells the story of humankind's continual rebellion against God. Genesis tells of Adam and Eve's disobedience, thus beginning humanity's tragic descent into sin. This pattern is repeated in the rest of the Pentateuch, in the Historical Books, and to the end of the Old Testament.

Israel's unfaithfulness was a serious matter because the people's sin separated them from God—and from His mission (Isaiah 59:2). Their unfaithfulness disqualified them as God's representatives to the Gentile nations (43:10, 12; 44:8). Because of their continued rebellion, Israel failed to give a witness to the nations, as God had required (26:18).

The Old Testament also tells how for hundreds of years God sent prophets to call Israel to repent. If Israel did not repent, they would suffer judgment and exile from the Promised Land (Jeremiah 7:22–26). There were moments in Israel's history when the people did repent and turn back to God. Each time, however, their repentance was sadly only temporary, and eventually they again turned away from God. This repeated rebellion against God grieved the Holy Spirit (Isaiah 63:10). Finally, God judged Israel, allowing the Jews to be taken into captivity (2 Kings 17:6–20; 2 Chronicles 36:11–21).

A New Heart

While Israel was in Babylonian captivity, the Spirit of God began to speak through Ezekiel the prophet. Ezekiel foretold how the Lord would someday restore the nation and bring them back to the Promised Land. Ezekiel also emphasized the essential work of the Holy Spirit in this process.

Chapter 5 ~ The Missionary Spirit Reveals God's Mission

Ezekiel prophesied that God would purify Israel and bring them out of captivity. At that time, He would give Israel a new spirit and transform their hard hearts. This transformation would motivate them to serve and obey God (Ezekiel 11:17–20; 36:24–27). The transformation would come as a result of God placing His Holy Spirit in them: "I will put my Spirit in you and move you to follow my decrees and be careful to obey my laws" (36:27).

Ezekiel continued this theme in his vision of dry bones (Ezekiel 37:1–14). In the vision, Ezekiel saw a field scattered with dry bones, but God miraculously brought the bones together and put new flesh on them. Then, the Spirit of God entered them, and they came to life. The bones represented Israel, who was scattered and cut off from God (37:11–14). However, God would someday fill them with His Spirit and restore them to life (37:14). This vision was an illustration of a powerful transformation that God promised to accomplish by His Spirit.

It is important to understand that this transformation would occur at the time when God raised up a new Davidic king to reign over His people (Ezekiel 37:24–28). Ezekiel, like Isaiah, connected the coming Messiah with a promise that He would do a new work in His people by His Spirit. What is unique to Ezekiel's prophecy, however, is his emphasis on the transformation of the heart that the Spirit would perform.

Later in our study we will see that the work of the Holy Spirit in transforming the heart is essential for a person to know and serve God (Romans 8:9–11). When people repent and turn to God, the Holy Spirit gives them new life in Christ and places them into the kingdom of God (John 3:3–8; see also 2 Corinthians 5:17). When we study the work of the Spirit in the New Testament, we will examine more fully the work of the Spirit in the process of salvation and sanctification.

A New Heart and the Mission of God

The Spirit's promise to restore Israel to the Promised Land and enable them to walk in obedience to God's law was part of God's plan for Israel to be a light to the nations. The prophet repeatedly stated that the reason God was going to do this work in Israel was because He wanted the nations to know Him (Ezekiel 36:22–23, 35–36, 38).

God was certainly concerned for Israel, but He was also concerned for the nations around Israel. These nations witnessed what God was doing for Israel. If He did not deliver His people, those nations might conclude that the God of Israel was powerless and not worthy to be served.

Therefore, God promised to deliver Israel and bring them back to their land. However, for Israel to become the testimony to the nations that God intended them to be, their hearts needed to be changed. Only then could they serve and obey God and His mission as they should (Ezekiel 36:23–27). The gift of the Spirit would prepare God's people to be His witnesses. One way to do this would be through their faithful obedience to Him.

THE SPIRIT WILL EMPOWER THE MESSIAH'S PEOPLE TO PROCLAIM GOD'S WORD

The Old Testament prophets spoke of another missionary purpose of the gift of the Holy Spirit to God's people. They prophesied that sometime in the future, God was going to fill His people with the Holy Spirit and empower them to proclaim His Word. This is an essential aspect of the Spirit's role in fulfilling the mission of God. Two prophecies point to this missionary purpose. One was given by Isaiah and another by Joel.

Isaiah's Prophecy Concerning Spirit-Empowerment

Through Isaiah, God made a promise to the Messiah and to His people: "My Spirit, who is on you, will not depart from you, and my words that I have put in your mouth will always be on your lips, on the lips of your children and on the lips of their descendants—from this time on and forever" (Isaiah 59:21).

In this promise, God revealed that the Holy Spirit would be the source of the Messiah's message. Notice that this promise of empowerment for proclamation is also for the Messiah's children (ie. his spiritual descendants who are saved through his suffering and death, 53:4-7, 10) The words that the Spirit would put in the mouth of the Messiah would also be put in the mouths of the Messiah's children (59:21). Thus, both the Messiah and His children would proclaim the good news of God's salvation in the power and anointing of the Holy Spirit (see also Isaiah 61:1–2; Luke 4:18–20; Acts 1:8).

Joel's Prophecy Concerning Spirit-Empowerment

Another important prophecy concerning the Spirit's empowering work in the lives of God's people is found in Joel 2:28–32. A warning of a coming day of judgment precedes this prophecy. Joel called this day of judgment *"the day of the LORD"* (1:15; 2:1, 11, 31; 3:14, emphasis added). If Israel and the nations refused to repent and turn back to God, judgment would surely come upon them. Joel further announced a second day of judgment. This time judgment would come on all nations. Joel called this day of judgment *"the great and dreadful day of the LORD"* (2:31; 3:1–2, emphasis added). This time the prophet was speaking of the final judgment at the end of history.

Between these two "days" of judgment, God promised to do a marvelous thing: "And afterward, I will pour out my Spirit on all people. Your sons and daughters will prophesy, your old men will dream dreams, your young men will see visions. Even on my servants, both men and women, I will pour out my Spirit in those days" (Joel 2:28–29). This mighty outpouring of the Spirit would enable God's people to participate effectively in His mission by empowering them to proclaim His Word.

Many years before Joel's prophecy, Moses declared, "I wish that all the LORD's people were prophets and that the LORD would put His Spirit on them!" (Numbers 11:29). In effect, Joel was saying the day would come when Moses' wish would come true. God would bring it about by His Spirit. In that day, He would pour out His Spirit on all His people, and as a result, they would all become prophets!

This is a wonderful promise because, before Pentecost, the ability to speak the words of God was given only to certain leaders and prophets of Israel. However, Joel promised that the day would come when all of God's people would become His prophets. God would reveal himself to them and speak through them.

Joel further revealed the purpose of this universal outpouring of the Spirit; it was to accomplish God's mission of bringing salvation to the world. This outpouring of the Spirit, and the resulting Spirit-empowered proclamation of God's prophetic people, would result in a great harvest of souls. At that time, "everyone who calls on the name of the LORD will be saved" (Joel 2:32). This future outpouring of the Spirit would occur to bring salvation to many before God's judgment comes on the world.

Later in our study, we will examine how Joel's prophecy was initially fulfilled on the Day of Pentecost when God poured out His Spirit on the church in Jerusalem. On that day, Peter quoted this prophecy of Joel, announcing that the outpouring of the Spirit on the 120 disciples marked the beginning of the fulfillment of that promise (Acts 2:17–21). We will discover how the book of Acts directly links Joel's prophecy to God's mission to call to himself a people from every nation on earth (1:8; 28:28).

Chapter 5 ~ The Missionary Spirit Reveals God's Mission

THE OLD TESTAMENT BELIEVER'S EXPERIENCE OF THE SPIRIT

In Chapter 4, we looked at how by His Spirit, God formed Israel as a nation. We also saw how He anointed certain prophets, kings, builders, and other leaders to enable Israel to accomplish the mission He had given them. In this chapter, we have further discovered how the Old Testament prophets looked for a day when, by His Spirit, God would do a new work in and through His people. It would be a work of transformation and empowering. In doing this, God would enable all His people to participate in the Spirit-empowered proclamation of His Word.

However, other questions arise: What about those Old Testament believers who were not leaders or prophets? Did they also experience the work of the Spirit in their lives? And if they did, in what ways did they experience the Spirit? Moreover, how does their experience compare with that of believers in the New Testament? These questions have caused much discussion among Bible students, resulting in different ideas on the subject.

To answer these questions properly, we must first understand the different works of the Spirit in Scripture. Three major works of the Spirit are the following:

- *Salvation:* The Spirit convicts people of their sin, draws them to God, and regenerates them, making them children of God.
- *Sanctification:* The Spirit transforms and strengthens believers, giving them power to live holy, Christ-like lives.
- *Empowerment:* The Spirit empowers believers and gives them gifts to fill certain roles and to perform certain tasks for Him.

Our study has shown that, in the Old Testament, the Spirit only empowered certain leaders and at certain times. The prophets, however, looked forward to the coming of the Messiah as the time when God would pour out the Spirit generously on all of God's people, enabling them to live for Him and to effectively participate in His mission. In the New Testament, we learn more fully how the Spirit works in regeneration and sanctification. The Old Testament gives little information concerning the work of the Spirit in this area of a believer's life. This fact makes it difficult to arrive at any clear conclusion concerning the work of the Spirit in the lives of all Old Testament saints.

There are, nevertheless, some indications of how the Spirit was at work in their lives. For instance, we know that the Spirit was continually present in Israel, working to prepare a people who were holy and dedicated to God. For example, even though Ezekiel looked forward to the Spirit transforming hearts, it is evident that God desired for the people of Ezekiel's day to repent. He therefore offered them the chance to experience the transforming work of the Spirit in their own hearts (Ezekiel 18:31).

We also know that the Hebrew prophets sometimes called on God's people to "circumcise their hearts" (Deuteronomy 10:16; Jeremiah 4:4). This is a figurative way of saying that people needed to humble their hearts before God and repent of their sins. If they would do this, Moses declared that "the LORD your God will circumcise your hearts...so that you may love him with all your heart and with all your soul, and live" (Deuteronomy 30:6). In other words, we first "circumsize" our own hearts, that is we humble ourselves before God in faith and repentance. In response, God, by His Spirit, completes the work by transforming us and enableing us to live for Him.

Two New Testament passages support this Old Testament understanding of the Spirit's work. In Acts 7:51, Stephen accused the Jewish Sanhedrin of having uncircumcised hearts and ears. This was because they were resisting the Holy Spirit just as their forefathers had done. Then in Romans 2:29, Paul declared that true circumcision is "inward," that it is "circumcision of the heart, by the Spirit."

These New Testament verses affirm that the Holy Spirit was at work in the hearts of sincere believers even in the Old Testament. He was actively working to transform the hearts of those people who wanted to obey God. The Old Testament does emphasize, however, that the future work of the Spirit would be much greater. In the time of the coming Messiah, the Spirit would indwell and empower all of God's people to participate in His mission in a way never experienced by the Old Testament believers (John 14:17; Acts 1:8).

IMPLICATIONS AND APPLICATIONS

This chapter has focused on several Old Testament prophecies concerning a future work of the Spirit in the lives of God's chosen people. The prophets declared that this work of the Spirit would enable God's people to live for Him and advance His mission on earth. We have also learned how the prophets foretold a coming Son of David, the Messiah, who would be enabled by the Holy Spirit to accomplish His God-given mission. The Hebrew prophets also spoke of a day when God would pour out His Spirit on all the Messiah's people. As a result, His Spirit would transform their hearts and empower them to join in the Messiah's mission of proclaiming the gospel to all nations.

These Old Testament prophecies serve as an important background to what we will study about the work of the Spirit in the New Testament. They announce the future work of the Spirit, and they help us understand the vital role that the Holy Spirit plays in accomplishing God's mission to save the nations.

Our study of the work of the Spirit in the Old Testament showed us how God was displeased with Israel's resistance to His mission and His Spirit. Israel's failure to represent God to the nations serves as a warning to us today. We should take care that we do not follow their bad example. God's purpose for His people has always been for them to serve Him in holiness and stand as His witnesses to the nations. Like the nation of Israel, if we fail to walk in obedience to God and serve Him and His purposes, we too will be judged.

The great need of the Old Testament believers was to experience the presence and power of the Holy Spirit. Only then could they fully serve God. For this reason, God promised that one day He would pour out His Spirit on all His people, enabling them to obey Him fully and proclaim His Word to the nations. We are living in that day. As God's representatives to the nations we too must humbly seek God and be filled with the Spirit.

Through His death and resurrection, Christ fulfilled the redemptive promises of the Old Testament. These included the promise of a worldwide outpouring of the Spirit on God's people. This promise was first fulfilled at Pentecost and continues to be fulfilled today. We will learn more about this in coming chapters. Today God requires us to humble ourselves before Him, repent, and receive the promise of the Father (Joel 2:28–29; Acts 1:4–5; 2:38–39). If we will do this, we can experience the living and powerful presence of the Spirit as He purifies and empowers us for God's mission.

Chapter 5 ~ The Missionary Spirit Reveals God's Mission

Questions for Discussion and Reflection

1. The Old Testament contains prophesies that the Messiah would be empowered by the Spirit to establish God's eternal kingdom. How are these prophecies important for the church today?

2. How are the prophecies concerning the work of the Spirit in the Messiah shown to be fulfilled in the stories concerning Christ in the four Gospels?

3. The Old Testament contains prophesies that the people of the Messiah would also be empowered by the Spirit. In what way are these prophecies connected to the story of the church in the book of Acts as well as the church today?

4. According to Old Testament prophecies what are the two primary things the Holy Spirit will empower God's people to do? How do these relate to us?

5. Is it or is it not possible that true believers in the Old Testament were born again by the Spirit in the same way that the New Testament describes (see John 3:2-8)? Explain your answer.

Chapter 5 ~ The Missionary Spirit Reveals God's Mission

~ Part Three ~

The Missionary Spirit in the New Testament

~ CHAPTER 6 ~

THE MISSIONARY SPIRIT IN JESUS

Jesus Christ is the central figure of Scripture. The entire Bible focuses our attention on Him. This is especially true for the New Testament. It presents Jesus as the Son of God who became a man to do His Father's will and advance His mission. Through His life, death, and resurrection, Christ opened the door for all humanity to be redeemed. Now, through repentance from sin and faith in Him as Lord and Savior, anyone can enter God's kingdom (Luke 1:33, 35). It is fitting then that the writer of Hebrews challenges us to fix our eyes on Jesus, "the pioneer and perfecter of faith" (Hebrews 12:2).

In the Gospels, we discover that Jesus is unique among men. He is the perfect human who never sinned (Hebrews 4:15). He perfectly fulfilled the mission that the Father sent Him to accomplish (John 17:4; 19:30), and He made the way for all people to find forgiveness from sin (Matthew 1:21; 26:28; John 1:29). Jesus then commissioned His church to carry this message to the world in the power of the Holy Spirit (Mark 16:18; Luke 24:47–49; Acts 1:4–5, 8).

The Bible teaches that Jesus was, is, and will forever be fully God. Yet, the Bible also teaches that the eternal Son of God willingly became a man in order to carry out the Father's mission. Paul wrote that Jesus, "who, being in very nature God, did not consider equality with God something to be used to his own advantage; rather, he made himself nothing by taking the very nature of a servant, being made in human likeness" (Philippians 2:6–7). In other words, when Jesus came to earth, He willingly laid aside His rights and powers as God and lived as a true human being. The life He lived and the works He did were not accomplished in His own divine power but in the power of the Holy Spirit. As He began His ministry, Jesus testified that the Spirit of the Lord was on Him, anointing Him to carry out His ministry (Luke 4:18–19).

From the moment of Jesus' conception and birth until His death, resurrection, and ascension to heaven, the Spirit worked in Jesus' life. In this chapter, we will learn some important lessons about how the Spirit worked in the life of Jesus and how the Spirit wants to work in our lives today as disciples of Jesus who join Him in advancing the mission of God.

THE SPIRIT IN JESUS' EXEMPLARY LIFE

The Spirit in Jesus' Birth and Early Years

Both Matthew and Luke highlight the fact that the conception and birth of Jesus were miracles of the Holy Spirit (Matthew 1:18; Luke 1:34–35). The angel told Mary that, because she had conceived by the Holy Spirit, the child would be holy and would be called "the Son of God" (Luke 1:35). So from the first moment of His life, the Holy Spirit was working to prepare Jesus for His mission.

After His birth, the Holy Spirit guided Jesus' growth and development. Isaiah prophesied that "the Spirit of the LORD will rest on Him—the spirit of wisdom and of understanding" (Isaiah 11:2). It is therefore not surprising that Luke mentioned twice how Jesus grew in wisdom, with the grace and favor of God on Him (Luke 2:40, 52). At just twelve years of age, Jesus astounded the teachers in the temple with His wisdom and understanding of the Word of God (2:41–50).

The Spirit Prepared the Way for Jesus' Ministry

God sent John the Baptist to prepare the way for Christ's ministry. He told the people to repent and announced that the time had come for the kingdom of God to be established (Matthew 3:1–2; Luke 3:2–3). Like other Old Testament prophets before him, John foretold the arrival of the Messiah. However, John had the unique privilege of being the forerunner of Christ (Mark 1:2–3; Luke 3:4–6).

John's ministry was effective, and many people responded by repenting, confessing their sins, and being baptized in water (Matthew 3:5–6; Mark 1:5). Luke tells us that John ministered so powerfully because he was filled with the Holy Spirit. In fact, he was filled with the Holy Spirit while still in his mother's womb (Luke 1:15–17). The Holy Spirit played the defining role in the life and ministry of John the Baptist as He did with all the prophets (2 Peter 1:21).

John's message about the coming Messiah included an important new revelation. He said that Jesus would baptize people with (or in) the Holy Spirit. This important truth is found in each of the Gospels (Matthew 3:11; Mark 1:8; Luke 3:16; John 1:33). Matthew and Luke record John as announcing that Jesus would baptize in the Holy Spirit *and fire,* while Mark and John only mention baptizing in the Holy Spirit.

Scholars argue over whether baptism in the Holy Spirit and baptism in fire are the same or different baptisms.[17] Jesus, however, clearly taught that the baptism in the Holy Spirit refers to God's promise to pour out His Spirit on all His people to empower them as

---

[17] For an examination of differing interpretations concerning "baptism in fire" see: Horton, *What the Bible Says About the Holy Spirit,* 84–89.

His witnesses (Acts 1:4–8; compare 2:16–18). The baptism in fire likely refers to the final judgment of unbelievers (Matthew 13:40–42; 25:41; Revelation 20:15).

In the New Testament, fire is often used in the sense of judgement, and this is clearly the case in the verse following John the Baptist's declaration that Jesus would baptize with the Holy Spirit and fire (see Matthew 3:12 and Luke 3:17). Additionally, John, like other Old Testament prophets and the Jews of his day, viewed the coming of the Messiah as one event both to save His people and to judge the world. He did not understand the two stages in the coming of Christ with a long gap of time in between. This is possibly why later, when he was in prison, John sent word to ask Jesus if He was the Messiah or if they should wait for another to come after Him (Matthew 11:2–3; Luke 7:18–19).

In his preaching, John the Baptist summarized the primary goals of Jesus' ministry. First, Jesus would take away the sin of the world (John 1:29). Second, He would baptize His followers in the Holy Spirit (1:33). Jesus advanced God's mission by providing forgiveness of sins through His death and resurrection. He continues to advance the mission by baptizing His disciples in the Holy Spirit to enable them to proclaim the good news to the world (Acts 1:8; compare Luke 24:48–49).

The Spirit Empowered Jesus for Ministry

How important do you think it is to be empowered by the Holy Spirit for ministry? Jesus' life and ministry demonstrate that it is of utmost importance. Before Jesus began His public ministry, He was first anointed with the Holy Spirit. Each of the four Gospels records how the Spirit came on Jesus immediately after He was baptized in water (Matthew 3:16; Mark 1:10; Luke 3:21–22; John 1:32). This was a defining moment in Jesus' life. It was the moment when the Holy Spirit anointed and empowered Him to carry out His mission.

Once the Spirit came on Him, Jesus immediately began his ministry (Luke 3:23). Luke says that He then "returned to Galilee in the power of the Spirit" (4:14). He went to His hometown of Nazareth, and on the Sabbath, He went into the synagogue and read the prophecy of Isaiah 61:1–2 announcing:

> The Spirit of the Lord is on me, because he has anointed me to proclaim good news to the poor. He has sent me to proclaim freedom for the prisoners and recovery of sight for the blind, to set the oppressed free, to proclaim the year of the Lord's favor. (Luke 4:18–19)

Then, speaking of himself, Jesus announced, "Today this scripture is fulfilled in your hearing" (4:21). Thus, the Spirit of the Lord came on Jesus to anoint Him to proclaim the gospel and carry out His mission of providing salvation for the world.

As we have already stated, Jesus chose not to minister from His own divine power. To become our Savior, He needed to identify fully with our humanity (Hebrews 2:14–18). This means that as a man, He needed to be filled with the Spirit to carry out His redemptive mission. In fulfilling this mission, He was led by the Spirit (Luke 3:21–22; 4:1), proclaimed the gospel in the power of the Spirit (4:18), and healed the sick and drove out demons by the power of the Spirit (Matthew 12:22, 28).

In other words, everything Jesus did in His ministry, He did through the enablement of the Holy Spirit. Recognizing this fact, the apostle Peter declared that "God anointed Jesus of Nazareth with the Holy Spirit and power, and…he went around doing good and healing all who were under the power of the devil, because God was with him" (Acts 10:38). Jesus commanded His disciples to go and proclaim the same message He proclaimed (Matthew 4:17; 10:7; Luke 9:2; 24:47–48), to perform the same miracles He performed (Matthew 10:1, 8; Luke 9:1–2; 10:1, 9), and to do this in the same power of the Holy Spirit that enabled Him (Luke 24:49; Acts 1:4–5, 8).

This understanding of how Jesus ministered as a man empowered by the Holy Spirit, and how He passed His ministry on to His disciples, has profound and continuing implications for those of us who have chosen to follow Him. It means that He is our example of how we should live lives that are pleasing to God. It further means that Jesus is our example of how we can effectively participate in God's mission. Like Him, we must pursue our ministries in the power of the Holy Spirit. To do this, we must be baptized in the Holy Spirit and daily walk and minister in the Spirit's power.

The Spirit Enabled Jesus to Live a Sin-Free Life

The New Testament declares that Jesus lived a sinless life (Hebrews 4:15). How did He accomplish that? He did it as a human being just like us. He was "tempted in every way just as we are—yet he did not sin" (4:15), and "he himself suffered when he was tempted" (2:18). So what made the difference in Jesus' life that enabled Him to live without sin?

The Gospels of Matthew, Mark, and Luke all say that after Jesus' baptism, the Spirit led Him into the desert to be tempted by the devil for forty days. During that time, Jesus sought communion with God through fasting and prayer. At the end of the forty days, when Jesus was hungry and physically weakened, the devil came against Him and began to tempt Him (Matthew 4:1–3; Mark 1:12–13; Luke 4:1–2).

Three times the enemy attacked Him, and three times Jesus overcame the temptation in the power of the Spirit. Luke emphasized this point by stating both at the beginning and end of the temptation passage that Jesus was moving in the power of the Spirit. Soon after His baptism and empowering by the Spirit, Jesus "was led by the Spirit into the wilderness, where…he was tempted by the devil" (Luke 4:1). Then, following His temptation, "Jesus returned to

Galilee in the power of the Spirit" (4:14). It is logical to assume then that during His time in the wilderness, Jesus continued to move in the power of the Holy Spirit.

Further, Luke showed how Jesus responded to each temptation by counteracting Satan's lies with a declaration of the truth of God's Word. Pentecostal theologian French Arrington wrote that, in this way, Jesus gave us "a pattern by which Christians should meet temptation. By the power of the Spirit and by using Scripture, we must face Satan in the same way as he did."[18] Jesus' example demonstrates that the key to living free of sin is to remain full of the Holy Spirit and to stay continually focused on the truth of God's Word.

THE SPIRIT IN JESUS' POWERFUL TEACHING

The Spirit Enabled Jesus to Teach with Power and Authority

Jesus spent much of His approximately three years of ministry teaching God's Word. The Gospels often describe how His teaching amazed people. Unlike other religious leaders, He taught with authority and power (Matthew 7:28; Mark 1:22, 27; 11:18; Luke 4:32). His teaching was so powerful that people declared, "No one ever spoke the way this man does" (John 7:46).

One source of Jesus' powerful teaching was the anointing of the Holy Spirit that rested on His ministry. In his Gospel, Luke emphasized that after Jesus was filled with the Spirit at His baptism, He "returned to Galilee in the power of the Spirit" (Luke 4:14). Luke then added that Jesus "was teaching in their synagogues, and everyone praised him" (4:15). On another occasion while Jesus was teaching the people of Judea and Jerusalem, "the power of the Lord

---

[18] French L. Arrington, "Luke," in *Life in the Spirit New Testament Commentary*, ed. French L. Arrington and Roger Stronstad (Grand Rapids, MI: Zondervan, 1999), 411.

was with Jesus to heal the sick" (5:17). Luke thus connected the power of the Spirit with Jesus' teaching ministry. The book of Acts informs us that everything Jesus taught and commanded was through the Holy Spirit—even after His resurrection until the day He was taken up to heaven (Acts 1:1–2).

Because He spoke by the Spirit, Jesus could declare, "My teaching is not my own. It comes from the one who sent me" (John 7:16). He could truthfully say, "The words I have spoken to you—they are full of the Spirit and life" (6:63). As a result of the Spirit's anointing, Jesus' teaching transformed those He taught.

Only God's Word inspired by God's Spirit can bring life to dying people. The world desperately needs God's Word, and Jesus is our example of how we need to deliver it to them. His example of Spirit-anointed teaching points to our continued need today to be filled with the Spirit. Only then will we be able to teach God's Word powerfully as He did. Only then will lives be transformed.

The Missio-Pneumatological Themes in Jesus' Teaching

One essential facet of God's mission is that He established an eternal kingdom over which His anointed Servant, the Son of David, will rule (see 1 Chronicles 17:11–14; Luke 1:31–33). That is why Jesus began His ministry by announcing "the good news of the kingdom of God" (Luke 4:43; 8:1; 16:16; compare Matthew 4:23; 9:35; Mark 1:15). With these words, Jesus summarized His message. In teaching the people about the kingdom of God, He showed how the Spirit of God works to advance God's mission in the earth. Let us look at some of the *missio-pneumatological*[19] themes in Jesus' teaching.

---

[19] *Missio-pneumatological* is a term that refers to the work of the Holy Spirit in advancing the mission of God in the earth.

Entering the Kingdom of God by the Spirit

One vital missionary work of the Spirit is to incorporate people into the kingdom of God through spiritual rebirth. Jesus declared this work of the Spirit by explaining that "no one can see the kingdom of God unless they are born again" and "no one can enter the kingdom of God unless they are born of water and the Spirit" (John 3:3, 5).

When someone repents of their sin, puts their faith in Christ, and chooses to follow Him as Lord, the Spirit of God does a work of spiritual regeneration in that person's heart. As a result, they are made spiritually alive. They become a child of God and a citizen of His kingdom (John 1:12–13). In Chapter 8, we will study more in depth about the new-birth experience when we study the work of the Spirit in regeneration.

Advancing the Kingdom of God by the Power of the Spirit

We have discussed how God's mission involves the establishment of His kingdom. However, the Bible also reveals that there is another kingdom. This kingdom is led by Satan and opposes the advancement of God's kingdom (Ephesians 6:11–12). John wrote that "the whole world is under the control of the evil one" (1 John 5:19; compare Matthew 4:8–9; Luke 4:5–6). Consequently, every person who is not a part of the kingdom of God is a captive to sin, death, and the power of Satan (Hebrews 2:14–15).

Nevertheless, Jesus declared that those who are in captivity can be set free by the power of the Holy Spirit. One of the reasons Jesus was anointed by the Spirit was to "proclaim freedom for the prisoners" and to "set the oppressed free" (Luke 4:18). This promise certainly refers to those whom Satan holds in captivity through sin (John 8:34–47). Jesus liberated the captives from the power of Satan through this dynamic power of God's kingdom. He explained that He cast out demonic spirits by the power of the Holy Spirit and that this was an indication that the kingdom of God had come into their midst (Matthew 12:28; Luke 11:20).

One great missio-pneumatological theme in Jesus' teaching is that God continues to work through His Spirit-empowered people to set people free from the captivity of sin and Satan. For example, Paul testified that Jesus Christ appeared to him on the road to Damascus and called him to be a witness to the Gentiles. Jesus said to Paul, "I am sending you to them to open their eyes and turn them from darkness to light, and from the power of Satan to God, so that they may receive forgiveness of sins and a place among those who are sanctified by faith in me" (Acts 26:17–18). Today, God sends His people to do the same.

During the forty days between His death and resurrection, Jesus taught His disciples about the kingdom of God (Acts 1:3). He emphasized the necessity of their being empowered by the Holy Spirit to be able to advance His kingdom on the earth (1:4–5). He then promised them, "You will receive power when the Holy Spirit comes on you; and you will be my witnesses in Jerusalem, and in all Judea and Samaria, and to the ends of the earth" (1:8). Therefore, in His last words to His church before returning to heaven, Jesus stressed the mission and the need to be empowered by the Spirit to accomplish that mission.

The commission remains in effect today. As He did with His first disciples, Jesus sends us to boldly advance His kingdom in the face of satanic opposition. And as He did with the disciples, He promises that the Spirit's power will enable us to accomplish the task. This power is available through an experience Jesus called the baptism in the Holy Spirit (Acts 1:4–5). In Part 4, when we study the topic of being empowered for ministry, we will discuss this experience in detail. For now, it is essential that we clearly understand Jesus' teaching that the kingdom of God advances against the kingdom of Satan by the power of the Holy Spirit. This understanding will serve as a theological foundation on which we can build a practical model of Spirit-empowered mission. It will help us understand the practical necessity for every believer to be empowered by the Spirit.

Proclaiming the Gospel of the Kingdom by the Power of the Spirit

Another missio-pneumatological theme that we can learn from Jesus' teaching on the Holy Spirit is Spirit-empowered proclamation of the gospel of the kingdom. Jesus went around preaching the good news about the kingdom of God (Matthew 4:23; 9:35; Mark 1:14; Luke 8:1). In doing this, He announced that the time had come for the kingdom of God to be established. The people therefore needed to "repent and believe the good news!" (Mark 1:15).

Once when the people of Capernaum wanted to keep Jesus from leaving them, He responded by declaring, "I must proclaim the good news of the kingdom of God to the other towns also, because that is why I was sent" (Luke 4:43; compare Mark 1:38).

The Holy Spirit empowered Jesus to powerfully proclaim the gospel of the kingdom. Soon after His baptism in the Jordan River, Jesus explained why the Spirit had come on Him. He said, "The Spirit of the Lord is on me because he has anointed me to proclaim good news" (Luke 4:18). In this declaration, Jesus explained that the primary purpose of the anointing of the Holy Spirit is to enable us to effectively proclaim the gospel to the lost. Jesus has assigned to His church the principal task of witness to the world (Luke 24:48; Acts 1:8). This task demands that we join in the work of proclaiming the gospel of the kingdom to the nations (Matthew 24:14; Mark 16:15).

The Spirit powerfully anointed Jesus to preach the gospel. Jesus then turned to His disciples and told them that they would need that same power if they were to effectively proclaim the gospel to the lost. The same is true today. If we are to effectively proclaim the good news to lost people at home and around the world, we must be empowered by God's Spirit.

THE SPIRIT IN JESUS' MIGHTY WORKS

Miracles and Demonic Deliverance by the Power of the Spirit

The Gospel of Luke identifies Jesus as a prophet who was powerful in both "word *and deed*" (Luke 24:19; emphasis added). Everywhere Jesus ministered, He performed miraculous works. The four Gospels together record details of 35 miracles Jesus performed. This includes 17 healings, 6 expulsions of demonic spirits, 9 miracles of nature, and 3 people raised from the dead (repeated instances of the same miracle in parallel passages not included). In addition, there are numerous passages that describe how Jesus healed and delivered on many more occasions than those specifically mentioned.[20] As He did with the Old Testament prophets, the Spirit enabled Jesus both to proclaim God's message and to perform miraculous works. Jesus performed all His mighty works through the anointing of the Spirit.

One time, people brought a man to Jesus who was both blind and deaf. The man's condition was caused by an evil spirit (Matthew 12:22–24; Luke 11:14–15). Jesus healed the man by casting the demon spirit out of him. When Jesus did that, some hostile Jewish religious leaders criticized Him, saying, "It is only by Beelzebul, the prince of demons, that this fellow drives out demons" (Matthew 12:24; compare Luke 11:15). Jesus countered by pointing out that if this was the case, Satan was fighting against himself and his kingdom would surely fall. He then declared, "If it is by the Spirit of God that I drive out demons, then the kingdom of God has come upon you" (Matthew 12:28). Here, Jesus revealed that His miracles were evidence that the kingdom of God had indeed arrived. He also revealed that the Holy Spirit was the source of His kingdom power. The Spirit enabled Him to perform His mighty works of healing and deliverance.

---

[20] See Matthew 4:23–24; 8:16; 9:35; 12:15; 14:14, 36; 15:30; 19:2; Mark 1:34; 3:10; 6:56; Luke 4:40; 5:15; 6:18–19; 9:11.

Those of us who follow Christ and have joined Him in His mission must understand this powerful truth; it is the Spirit who enables. Further, we must understand the implications of this truth. Jesus once stated, "Whoever believes in me will do the works I have been doing, and they will do even greater things than these, because I am going to the Father" (John 14:12). He then explained what would happen when He met the Father: "And I will ask the Father, and he will give you another Helper, to be with you forever, even the Spirit of truth" (14:16–17). In other words, the Holy Spirit would be the Helper who would enable believers to do the works of Jesus.

Jesus intends for those who follow Him to continue His Spirit-empowered ministry until He returns. That ministry includes proclaiming the gospel and healing and delivering people from the power of Satan. This is why He gives us the same Holy Spirit who enabled Him to perform His might works.

Signs and Wonders as a Demonstration of the Kingdom of God

Signs and wonders were a significant part of Jesus' ministry. They validated His message and demonstrated that He was indeed the promised Messiah. They also showed that the kingdom of God had come and that His kingdom was more powerful than the kingdom of Satan. In his Gospel, John often used the word *sign* rather than *miracle* to describe Jesus' mighty works. He did this to emphasize the truth of Jesus' message and to call people to faith in Christ.[21]

Jesus intends for powerful demonstrations of the kingdom of God to continue through the church until He comes again. When He sent out His disciples to preach the good news, Jesus intended for them to minister in the same way they had seen Him minister. They were to proclaim the same gospel of the kingdom of God and call people to repentance (Matthew 10:7; Mark 6:12–13; Luke 9:2). Jesus further gave them power and authority over unclean spirits, and He instructed

---

[21] See John 2:11, 23; 4:54; 6:2, 14; 7:31; 12:18, 37; 20:30

the disciples to demonstrate the power of God's kingdom by healing the sick, casting out demon spirits, and even raising the dead just as He had done (Matthew 10:1, 8; Mark 3:14–15; 6:7; Luke 9:1–2).

Not only did Jesus give these instructions to the twelve apostles, but He also gave similar instructions to the seventy-two other disciples whom He sent out to preach (Luke 10:1–12). Jesus told them to "*heal* the sick…and *tell* them, 'The kingdom of God has come near to you'" (10:9, emphasis added). Jesus was commissioning them to challenge and defeat the kingdom of Satan in the same way that He had—by their words and deeds (Luke 10:19).

When Jesus sent out the seventy-two, He urged them, "Ask the Lord of the harvest, therefore, to send out workers into his harvest field" (Luke 10:2). This was necessary because "the harvest is plentiful, but the workers are few" (10:2). Further, every laborer who answers the call of Christ to go and proclaim the gospel must be empowered by the Spirit. Only then will they, like Jesus, be able to demonstrate the reality of the kingdom of God. For in the words of the apostle, "The kingdom of God is not a matter of talk but of power" (1 Corinthians 4:20).

Jesus' emphasis on demonstrating the power of the kingdom through signs and wonders is vital to the work of missions in Africa, where the reality and influence of the spirit world is evident everywhere. Just as in Jesus' day, demonic activity is widespread and is the source of many of the problems people face. The church must not draw back from this challenge. We must respond as Jesus responded. We must go out in the power and anointing of the Holy Spirit, and as Jesus instructed, we must "heal the sick who are there and tell them, 'The kingdom of God has come near to you'" (Luke 10:9).

Jesus' Warning Concerning Power and Priorities

As we seek to minister in the Spirit's power accompanied by miraculous signs, we must be careful to heed Jesus' warning to keep our focus and priorities in the right place. When the seventy-two returned to Jesus, they rejoiced. "Lord," they exclaimed, "even the demons submit to us in your name" (Luke 10:17). Jesus rejoiced with them and affirmed that He had indeed given them authority to overcome all the power of the enemy (10:18–19, 21). Then Jesus' mood changed, and He soberly warned them, "Do not rejoice that the spirits submit to you, but rejoice that your names are written in heaven" (10:20). We are to rejoice in what God has done for us, not what we have done for Him. God's greatest gift to His servants is not a powerful ministry; it is the gift of entrance into His eternal kingdom.

Just as in Jesus' day, Christian ministers in Africa today who are used mightily by the Spirit of God face a grave temptation. It is a temptation we must avoid at all costs. In Africa, people tend to show deep respect for those who demonstrate spiritual power. Because of this, people sometimes put their faith in the preacher rather than in God. As a result, some preachers have become arrogant and full of pride. Ministers of the gospel must be on constant guard against falling into the temptation of using miracles to glorify themselves rather than to glorify and advance God's kingdom.

When Jesus sent out the seventy-two on their mission, He spoke directly to this issue of the temptation for personal glorification. He told these disciples that they were not to move from house to house seeking attention and luxury treatment. Rather, when they were welcomed into a person's home to stay, they were to settle there for a while and eat whatever was set before them (Luke 10:7–8). Jesus knew the temptation they would face, so He instructed them to remain focused on the mission and not take advantage of the people's generosity. They were not to manipulate others for personal gain. In light of the mighty miracles the disciples performed, it is easy to imagine how they could have been tempted to take advantage of the people's gratitude.

Jesus gave the disciples strict orders. The disciples needed to ensure that Jesus' mission remained their priority, and they were not to seek excessive material benefits from the people. Rather, they were to be content with God's provision. Jesus' instructions are in stark contrast to a common situation in many churches today where leaders constantly manipulate their people by promising God's blessing if only the people will open their purses and give to the "man of God."

Jesus then pronounced judgment on the towns of Korazin, Bethsaida, and Capernaum because He had preached and worked miracles among them and yet they still refused to repent of their sins (Luke 10:13–15). He declared that these towns would face harsher judgment than other places that had not witnessed such miracles. This declaration informs both hearers and proclaimers of the gospel that miracles are not to be viewed as an end in themselves. Rather, they are meant to serve the greater goal of bringing people to repentance and commitment to God.

When people are healed and delivered by the power of the Holy Spirit, Christian workers must be quick to glorify God and call people to repentance and faith in Christ. Jesus was never satisfied with less than genuine repentance, and neither should we be today. Those who proclaim the gospel must always remember that signs and wonders are not poof of a successful ministry. The greatest proof is souls won for Christ.

THE SPIRIT IN JESUS' DEATH AND RESURRECTION

Every aspect of Jesus' life and ministry was directed by the Holy Spirit. This includes Jesus' death on the cross and His resurrection from the dead. These two great redemptive acts were the primary purpose for which God sent Jesus to the earth (Mark 10:45; John

12:27). Through His death and resurrection, salvation and forgiveness of sins have been made available to all people. The Holy Spirit enabled Jesus to accomplish all of this.

The writer of Hebrews states that it was "through the eternal Spirit" that Jesus shed His blood on the cross and offered himself to God as the perfect sacrifice for sin (Hebrews 9:14). This lets us know that the Holy Spirit was powerfully present during Jesus' crucifixion, enabling Him to endure the shame and suffering of the cross.

Then, three days later, the Holy Spirit raised Jesus from the dead. Paul explained how through the Holy Spirit, Jesus "was declared the Son of God with power by the resurrection from the dead" (Romans 1:4, NASB). Jesus' triumph over death and the grave was an important work of the Holy Spirit which proved that Jesus is indeed the powerful son of God. Paul later spoke of the Spirit "who raised Jesus from the dead" (8:11). That same Spirit is the one who will raise us from the grave when Jesus comes again. Even now, the powerful Spirit of God has raised us to new life in Christ.

During the forty days between His resurrection and ascension, Jesus continued to move in the power of the Holy Spirit. Luke tells us that during that time, Jesus gave "instructions through the Holy Spirit to the apostles he had chosen" (Acts 1:2). Thus in His birth, His life, His ministry, His death, His resurrection, and all the way up to the time of His ascension, Jesus lived in the power of the Holy Spirit and under His guidance.

THE SPIRIT IN JESUS' GREAT COMMISSION

The command Jesus gave to "go into all the world and preach the gospel to all creation" (Mark 16:15) and to "make disciples of all nations" (Matthew 28:19) is commonly referred to as the Great Commission. On several occasions between Christ's death and resurrection, He made declarations concerning this commission. The commission to be Christ's witnesses in the world is the ultimate purpose of the church.

As we prepare in the next chapter to consider the work of the Spirit in the ministry of the church, it is vital to recognize that Jesus highlighted the importance of the presence and power of the Spirit to enable the church for this mission. The presence and powerful work of the Spirit is the primary key to the effective ministry of the church.

The Great Commission in Matthew

Matthew's Gospel ends with Jesus commissioning the disciples to "go and make disciples of all nations" (Matthew 28:19). Jesus concludes this commission by promising, "Surely I am with you always, to the very end of the age" (28:20). This is a promise of the accompanying presence of the Holy Spirit who would remain and work with the disciples following Christ's ascension.

When Jesus initially sent out the disciples to bear witness for Him, He encouraged them not to be anxious even when they were persecuted or arrested. He told them not to worry because the Holy Spirit would be with them and would enable them to speak and bear witness even in those difficult times (Matthew 10:17–20). This promise of the presence and enablement of the Spirit remains to the end of the age (28:20) and is for all of Christ's followers who obey the Great Commission until Christ returns.

The Great Commission in Mark

Mark's Gospel ends with Jesus commissioning the disciples to "go into all the world and preach the gospel to all creation" (Mark 16:15). To those who accepted this commission, Jesus promised that miraculous signs would accompany and validate their ministry (16:17–18). Casting out demons, speaking in tongues, divine protection, and healing are miraculous signs that the Holy Spirit uses to open doors for the gospel. The Holy Spirit continues working today in the miraculous to open doors for the servants of God who proclaim the gospel to the lost world.

The Great Commission in Luke

Luke's Gospel tells of another occasion after the resurrection when Jesus commissioned His followers to witness to all nations about His death and resurrection and to declare that those who repent can receive forgiveness of sins (Luke 24:46–48). Jesus also immediately promised to fulfill a promise that His Father had made to clothe the disciples "with power from on high" (24:49). The promise of the Father is the promise to pour out the Holy Spirit to empower His people to be His witnesses (Joel 2:28–29; Acts 2:16–18). Jesus told the disciples to remain in Jerusalem until they received this promise. He was commanding them to make it their highest priority to be empowered by the Holy Spirit before engaging in the Great Commission. Receiving the promised empowerment of the Spirit should be a priority for every Christian to prepare them to engage in God's mission to bear witness for Christ.

The Great Commission in John

John's Gospel tells us that on the day Jesus rose from the dead, He appeared to His disciples and did two things. First, He commissioned them: "As the Father has sent me, I am sending you" (John 20:21). Second, "he breathed on them and said, 'Receive the Holy Spirit'" (20:22). Jesus transferred His mission to the church. Along with the mission, however, He also commanded the disciples to receive the Spirit. Christ's followers cannot carry out this mission without the power of the Holy Spirit.

It is not clear in this passage if something happened within the disciples at that moment. Possibly Jesus was simply preparing them for the outpouring of the Spirit that would happen on the Day of Pentecost. What is clear, however, is that Jesus once again connected

His mission to receiving the power of the Spirit. The success of the church in carrying out Christ's mission is tied to receiving the Holy Spirit.

IMPLICATIONS AND APPLICATIONS

We Can Have Confidence in the Work Jesus Accomplished

From beginning to end, the Holy Spirit played an essential role in the life and ministry of Jesus, who was anointed by the Spirit and lived His life under the Spirit's direction. The Old Testament prophets told how the Messiah would be uniquely anointed by the Spirit, and the Gospels show in detail how these prophecies were fulfilled.

The Spirit's work in and through Jesus serves as a powerful confirmation that He is truly the promised Messiah and that He accomplished His mission victoriously. The Spirit's crowning work of raising Jesus from the dead irrefutably demonstrates that Jesus is indeed who He claimed to be: the Son of God and the Savior of the world. Because of these things, we can place our full confidence in Christ as our Savior and anointed King.

We Can Follow Jesus' Spirit-Empowered Model for Missions

The work of the Spirit in Jesus' life and ministry has further implications for those who believe in Him and follow Him as Savior and Lord. Jesus' Spirit-empowered ministry stands as a perfect model of how God wants His followers to advance His kingdom and mission throughout the earth. The same power that rested on Jesus to help Him fulfill His mission can rest on us as we seek to further that same mission. God's Word promises us that power. By the power of the Spirit, we can advance the kingdom of God just like Jesus did through proclamation of the gospel and miraculous works (John 7:37–39; Acts 1:8; 2:17, 38–39).

When we read the Gospels, we not only read about what Jesus

did, but we also see an example of *what* Jesus wants us to do and *how* He wants us to do it. He sends us to proclaim the good news of the kingdom of God to all nations. As we go, we are to demonstrate the power of God's kingdom just as He did. He has promised us the power of the Holy Spirit to enable us for this task.

In our next chapter, we will examine how the Holy Spirit worked in the ministry of the early church. We will see that the early followers of Jesus Christ went out and continued the work that He began. If we will believe in Jesus' promise, commit ourselves to His mission, and seek to be filled with the Holy Spirit, we can continue Jesus' work in our day until the nations are won for Him.

Questions for Discussion and Reflection

1. How is Jesus a model for believers when they are faced with temptation to sin?

2. What are some of the ways Jesus modeled Spirit-empowered ministry?

3. How might we apply to ministry the principles found in the missio-pneumatological themes of Jesus' teaching?

4. How can we apply Jesus' model of Spirit-empowered ministry to the work of ministry and missions today?

5. Do you think there are church leaders today who fall into the temptation of abusing the miraculous power of the Holy Spirit? In light of Jesus' warning concerning power and priorities, how can we avoid this error?

6. How might an understanding of the work of the Spirit in all of Jesus' life influence our trust in Christ's redemptive mission and model for ministry?

~ CHAPTER 7 ~

THE MISSIONARY SPIRIT IN THE CHURCH

In the Old Testament, God chose for His Spirit to dwell among His people, first in the tabernacle and later in the temple in Jerusalem (Exodus 40:34–38; 1 Kings 8:10–11). God's presence in these special buildings, however, was a mere foreshadowing of His ultimate goal to dwell in and among His people.

The New Testament reveals that the church is the new temple in which the Spirit of God dwells (2 Corinthians 6:16). The church is not a building; it is the collective people of God. The Spirit indwells the church and desires to fill and empower each person in the church (1 Corinthians 3:16; 6:19).

This new "temple" of the Lord is not yet complete. God is in the process of building His church (Ephesians 2:19–22). As people repent of their sins and put their faith in Christ for salvation, the Holy Spirit baptizes them into the body of Christ, the church (1 Corinthians 12:13). They are added to the temple of the Lord and become "living stones" in God's ever-growing spiritual house (1 Peter 2:5). God's temple will only be complete when it includes people from "every tribe and language and people and nation" (Revelation 5:9; 7:9;

compare Matthew 24:14). Until that time, the church has a mission to fulfill.

Jesus transferred His mission to His church. However, He did not leave the church to accomplish the mission in its own power. Before returning to heaven, Jesus promised to send the Holy Spirit to empower the church to fulfill the mission (John 14:15–18). Then at Pentecost, Jesus poured out His Spirit on the church and launched it into its mission. Since that day, the Holy Spirit powerfully indwells the church. He has been diligently working through God's people to build the new temple of God.

In this chapter, we will examine how the Spirit of God works in and through the church to accomplish God's mission of preparing a people from all nations among whom He may dwell for all eternity (Revelation 21:3).

JESUS' FINAL COMMAND AND PROMISE

The Great Commission in Acts

As we saw in the last chapter, each of the four Gospels ends with the Great Commission. The book of Acts, however, *begins* with Jesus issuing His Great Commission. There is another interesting difference between the Gospels and Acts. The Gospels present the Great Commission followed by a promise of the Spirit's presence and power. The book of Acts, however, presents Christ's promise of the Spirit's power followed by Christ giving His Great Commission (Acts 1:4–5, 8). Commenting on this change in emphasis, Hodges explains:

> The missionary endeavor of preaching the gospel to the whole world could not be carried out simply as loyal obedience to the commands of Jesus. The apostles and early Christians needed an inward impulse—they must become co-laborers with God and find an inward compulsion for the fulfilling of this command.

This dynamic for world evangelism came on the Day of Pentecost.[22]

The gift of the Spirit is the essential link between the work of Jesus and the work of the church. While the Gospels tell what Jesus "began to do and to teach" (Acts 1:1), Acts shows how He *continued* to "do and teach" through His church; He did this by sending His Spirit to empower, motivate, and guide the church in its mission (2:33).

The Final Command: Unique and Timeless

Before Christ returned to heaven, He gave a final command for His disciples to wait in Jerusalem until they had received the promise of the Father and had been baptized in the Holy Spirit (Luke 24:49; Acts 1:4–5). This command is in one sense unique, but in another sense, it is timeless.

A Unique Command

Jesus' command to "wait" for the Spirit was unique for the apostles in that they were to wait because the Spirit had not yet been poured out. God in His sovereignty chose the Day of Pentecost to fulfill His promise to pour out the Spirit on the church (Acts 2:1–4). Since that day, the promised Holy Spirit is available to all believers, and no one is required to wait to receive the gift (Acts 2:38–39). Jesus has promised to give the Holy Spirit to any disciple who will ask in faith (Luke 11:1–10; Mark 11:24).

---

[22] Melvin L. Hodges, *A Theology of the Church and Its Mission: A Pentecostal Perspective* (Springfield, MO: Gospel Publishing House, 1977), 34.

A Timeless Command

In another sense, Jesus' command to wait is a timeless command with crucial implications for the church today. When Jesus gave the command, He was highlighting the importance of every Christian being filled with and empowered by the Holy Spirit.

Jesus had repeatedly spoken to His disciples about their mission to preach the gospel and establish the church among all nations. His disciples knew what they were supposed to do. However, knowing the mission did not ensure that they would succeed in fulfilling it. For that to happen, they would need to be empowered by the Holy Spirit. The same is true for us today. We must take Christ's final command seriously. We must also make it a priority to seek the presence and power of the Spirit in our lives. Only then will we be able to advance God's mission on the earth successfully.

The Promise of Power for Witness

After commanding His disciples to be baptized in the Holy Spirit, Jesus explained the purpose of the experience. He said, "You will receive power when the Holy Spirit comes on you; and *you will be my witnesses* in Jerusalem, and in all Judea and Samaria, and to the ends of the earth" (Acts 1:8, emphasis added). In this key verse, Jesus promised His followers that the power of the Holy Spirit would enable them to effectively carry out His mission at home and to the ends of the earth.

Scholars often cite Acts 1:8 as the key verse to the book of Acts. However, they have often missed that this verse is also the key to effective evangelism and missions. With these words, Jesus identified why He made it a priority that every disciple be baptized in the Holy Spirit. The missionary Spirit of God is the source of God's power for effective witness. We receive this power for the mission when we are baptized in and filled with the Holy Spirit, just like the disciples in the early church.

Chapter 7 ~ The Missionary Spirit in the Church

PENTECOST: THE DAY GOD FIRST EMPOWERED THE CHURCH FOR HIS MISSION

The Spirit Is Poured Out on a Praying Church

The disciples obeyed Jesus' command to wait for the coming of the Spirit. However, they did not wait passively. Scripture says that "they all joined together constantly in prayer" (Acts 1:14) and "stayed continually at the temple, praising God" (Luke 24:53). They surely remembered Jesus' promise: "How much more will your Father in heaven give the Holy Spirit to those who ask him!" (Luke 11:13). Their response shows they understood that they were to prayerfully seek until the promise was fulfilled. Throughout the New Testament, prayer is closely associated with the working of the Spirit.[23] People received the Spirit in response to prayer. It is the same today; the Spirit still works powerfully in and through God's people when they seek Him in prayer.

On the Day of Pentecost, God fulfilled the promise Jesus had made in Acts 1:8. As the believers were gathered together in prayer and worship, God poured out His Spirit on them: "All of them were filled with the Holy Spirit and began to speak in other tongues as the Spirit enabled them" (Acts 2:4). Therefore, just as Jesus had promised, the Spirit came on the disciples to empower them as Christ's witnesses.

The Spirit Empowers the Church for Witness

The immediate result of the Spirit filling the believers at Pentecost was that they were empowered to speak in tongues "as the Spirit enabled them." However, speaking in tongues was not the only Spirit-empowered speech on that occasion. Soon, a large crowd

---

[23] Luke 3:21–22; 11:9–13; Acts 4:24, 29–31; 8:15; 9:17; Romans 8:26; Ephesians 6:18; Jude 20.

gathered to see what was happening. Peter stood and began to speak by the Spirit a second time. This time He did not speak in tongues but began to proclaim the good news about Christ in the common language (Acts 2:14–41). He was again speaking as the Spirit enabled him. Both times, Peter spoke by the power of the Spirit.

After hearing Peter's Spirit-empowered message, 3,000 people came to faith in Christ (Acts 2:41). This amazing response was not due to Peter's speaking ability; it was due to the Holy Spirit speaking through him to the people. Two evidences show this to be true.

The first evidence is the special word Luke used in Acts 2:14 to describe Peter's speaking. He wrote that Peter stood up and "addressed" the crowd. The word for "addressed" in the original Greek—*apophthengomai*—is generally used to indicate inspired speaking.[24] Luke had just used the same word in Acts 2:4 to describe how the Spirit "enabled" the disciples to speak in other tongues. He likely used this word twice to show that both the disciples' speaking in tongues in 2:4 and Peter's speaking to the crowd in 2:14 were inspired by the Spirit.

The second evidence that Peter's words were Spirit-empowered is what happened in the hearts of the people who heard his message. Acts 2:37 states, "When the people heard this, they were cut to the heart and said to Peter and the other apostles, 'Brothers, what shall we do?'" The Holy Spirit, who was inspiring Peter's words, brought powerful conviction to the hearts of the people. The conviction of the Spirit moved them to respond to the message (see John 16:8).

What an inspiring example of what God will do through His servants when they are empowered by His Spirit! Peter was an ordinary fisherman, yet the Holy Spirit enabled him to powerfully proclaim the good news of salvation in Christ. The result was a great harvest of souls for the kingdom of God. This story should inspire

---

[24] *Apophthengomai* appears only 3 times in the New Testament, all of which are in the book of Acts (Acts 2:4, 14; 26:25).

every follower of Christ to seek earnestly to be filled with the Spirit and empowered as Christ's witness.

The Missional Significance of Pentecost

At Pentecost, thousands of people gathered to see what was happening. God had poured out His Spirit on 120 of Jesus' followers, and they had begun to speak miraculously in several unlearned languages. Utterly amazed, the onlookers cried out, "What does this mean?" This is an important question. Since that day, many scholars have attempted to answer the question, "What is the meaning of Pentecost?" Often the Day of Pentecost is called the "birthday of the church." This view is held by many who view Pentecost as the day that Jesus followers were saved and born again by the Spirit. The correct answer, however, is the one Jesus gave.

Jesus Defined Pentecost Missionally

In His final words before returning to heaven, Jesus made clear the meaning of Pentecost. Speaking of what would happen on that day, He told His disciples, "You will receive power when the Holy Spirit comes on you; and you will be my witnesses in Jerusalem, and in all Judea and Samaria, and to the ends of the earth" (Acts 1:8).

Jesus revealed that Pentecost means that God has poured out His Spirit on the church to empower believers to take the gospel to the entire world. The baptism in the Holy Spirit, which Jesus promised and His followers received, prepared them to be Christ's witnesses "in Jerusalem…and to the ends of the earth." Said another way, God has given His missionary Spirit to His missionary people to fulfill His missionary plan to redeem all nations before Jesus comes again.

Peter Confirms Jesus' Definition

Jesus' missional definition of the purpose of Pentecost was further confirmed by Peter's response to the question of the crowd

(Acts 2:14-21). When the people who had gathered heard the believers speaking in other tongues, they asked, "What does this mean?" Peter answered that the Spirit's outpouring was a fulfilment of "what was spoken by the prophet Joel" (Acts 2:16). Hundreds of years earlier, the Holy Spirit had inspired the prophet to foretell that God would one day pour out His Spirit on *all* people, not just a select few as He had done before (Joel 2:28–32). Joel declared that in that day, all of God's people would prophesy. In other words, the day was coming when the Spirit would empower all of God's people to proclaim the message of salvation in Christ.

Joel further indicated that this Spirit-empowered proclamation would result in a great harvest of souls as people from all nations called on the name of the Lord (Joel 2:32; Acts 2:21). Peter reaffirmed Jesus' definition of Pentecost: The baptism in the Holy Spirit is an empowering experience given to enable all of God's people to effectively witness and proclaim the gospel to the lost.

THE SPIRIT'S PRESENCE AND POWER: THE KEY TO THE MISSIONARY SUCCESS OF THE CHURCH

The Holy Spirit is God's agent, sent by the Father and the Son to enable the church to fulfill its role in carrying out God's mission. The effectiveness of any church is determined by the degree to which it operates in the presence and power of the Spirit. The New Testament, especially the book of Acts, demonstrates that when the church commits itself to Christ and His mission and seeks the presence and power of the Holy Spirit, it will experience missionary success. Let us consider some of the primary ways the Holy Spirit works in and through the church.

The Spirit Enables the Proclamation of the Gospel

On the Day of Pentecost, anointed preaching of the Word resulted in many people coming to know Christ. However, this was not a unique event. Throughout the book of Acts, we read how the Holy Spirit continued to anoint the preaching of the gospel. God repeatedly poured the Spirit out on Christ's followers, and as a result, they proclaimed the Word of the Lord powerfully and the church grew exponentially.

In the days following Pentecost, the believers continued to pray, and God continued to fill them with His Spirit. On one occasion, after being threatened by local authorities, the church gathered for prayer. Acts 4:31 describes the result: "After they prayed, the place where they were meeting was shaken. And they were all filled with the Holy Spirit and spoke the word of God boldly." Luke then added, "With great power the apostles continued to testify to the resurrection of the Lord Jesus" (Acts 4:33). This pattern of Spirit-empowered proclamation continued throughout the book of Acts. Here are some more examples:

- Peter was again "filled with the Holy Spirit" and boldly proclaimed the gospel (Acts 4:8–12).
- Full of the Holy Spirit, Stephen preached with great wisdom and power (Acts 6:8–10, 15).
- Filled with the Holy Spirit, Philip proclaimed Christ to the Samaritans (6:3–5; 8:4–8).
- After being filled with the Spirit, Saul (Paul) immediately began to proclaim Jesus in the synagogues in Damascus (Acts 9:17–22).
- Scattered disciples proclaimed Christ in Antioch, and "the Lord's hand was with them" (Acts 11:19–21).

Spirit-empowered proclamation of the gospel was at the heart of the great missionary success of the early church. If the church today will be filled with the Spirit, it will be empowered to effectively proclaim the gospel to the lost.

The Spirit Validates the Gospel with Miraculous Signs

Jesus promised that those who faithfully preached the gospel would be enabled to perform miraculous signs in His name (Mark 16:15–18). These signs would witness to the truth of the gospel and to the reality of God's kingdom (Mark 16:19–20; Matthew 12:28). Christ's witnesses are enabled to do these works through the power of the Holy Spirit. Jesus declared that the Holy Spirit would testify about Him (John 15:26). Mighty works are one way the Spirit testifies that Christ is Lord and Savior.

Dynamis is the Greek word often translated "power" in our English New Testaments. It is sometimes translated "miraculous power," and in other cases, it is translated with the single word "miracle." Thus when Jesus promised in Acts 1:8, "You will receive power [*dynamis*] when the Holy Spirit comes on you," one implication is that the Holy Spirit will enable us to work miracles as part of our gospel witness. Consequently, Paul testified to the Romans that God had used him to lead Gentiles to faith and obedience "by the power of signs and wonders, through the power of the Spirit of God" (Romans 15:18–19).

The book of Acts is full of stories of Spirit-empowered people who worked miracles as part of their testimony for Christ. The apostles were surely empowered by the Spirit in this way (Acts 5:12, 16). We must remember, however, that others besides the apostles were also empowered. Stephen was "a man full of God's grace and power [who] performed great wonders and signs among the people" (Acts 6:8). Philip went to Samaria and proclaimed the gospel of Christ there: "When the crowds heard Philip and saw the signs he performed, they all paid close attention to what he said. For with shrieks, impure spirits came out of many, and many who were paralyzed or lame were healed" (Acts 8:6–7).

Miracles are also an important part of our gospel witness. Believers today need to seek to be empowered with the Spirit and to proclaim the gospel boldly. They must do this with the confidence that God will use them in signs and wonders. Such ministry will open doors for the proclamation of the gospel.

The Spirit Gives Strength and Courage to Witness

In the book of Acts, when disciples were filled with the Holy Spirit, a dramatic inner transformation took place. They were changed from weak and fearful disciples into brave and determined witnesses for Christ. Certainly, the resurrection of Christ was a great encouragement to them. However, even after the resurrection, the disciples were still not ready for the challenges they would encounter. This is why Jesus commanded them to wait in the city of Jerusalem until they were "clothed with power from on high" (Luke 24:49). However, when they were filled with the Spirit, they became courageous witnesses for Christ (Acts 4:8, 13). Even in the face of imprisonment, suffering, and death, they resolutely continued to preach the gospel (Acts 4:18–21; 5:41–42).

The same is true today. The Holy Spirit is our source for God's strength and courage. This is true for every person who desires to become an effective witness for the gospel. If we will diligently seek after God and be filled with the Spirit, He will strengthen us and empower us to witness for Christ boldly—even in the face of great difficulty.

The Spirit Enables the Church Facing Attacks from Without

Acts tells the amazing story of how the church advanced in obedience to the Great Commission. Soon after they began witnessing, however, serious attacks arose against them (Acts 8:1–3). These attacks would have destroyed any human organization, but the New Testament church was not merely a human organization. It was made up of transformed people who were committed to Christ and empowered by the Holy Spirit. Therefore, when they were attacked, they did not retreat but continued to witness in Christ's name. As a result, the church continued to grow and prosper. At times, Christ's disciples were persecuted and had to flee for their lives. However, this did not stop them from preaching the gospel with great boldness everywhere they went (Acts 8:4; 11:19; 14:5–7).

The founding of the church in Antioch is a prime example of this Spirit-given courage (Acts 11:19–24). Luke tells how certain Christians who fled the persecution in Jerusalem went to Antioch. There they began preaching the gospel to the Gentiles. Luke explained that "the Lord's hand was with them, and a great number of people believed and turned to the Lord" (Acts 11:21). As we learned in Chapter 2, the phrase "the hand of the Lord" speaks of the powerful working of the Holy Spirit. Even in times of persecution, the Holy Spirit empowered the church to advance and grow.

What an amazing and encouraging work of the Spirit! We should never be dismayed—no matter what difficulties or opposition we face. Rather, we should respond to persecution by praying as the early church prayed: "Now, Lord, consider their threats and enable your servants to speak your word with great boldness. Stretch out your hand to heal and perform signs and wonders through the name of your holy servant Jesus" (Acts 4:29–30). As He did with them, God will answer our prayers and pour out His Spirit on us, enabling us to continue proclaiming the gospel in power (4:31).

The Spirit Enables the Church Facing Attacks from Within

Some of the church's most serious attacks come from within its own ranks. Satan works to infiltrate the church and destroy its witness. He can do this by inspiring selfish, corrupt, and immoral acts in the lives of church members. The early church faced attacks like these. However, the Spirit empowered them to confront and overcome these internal challenges.

The story of Ananias and Sapphira is a prime example of this kind of threat to the church and its witness (Acts 5:1–11). This husband and wife attempted to deceive the leaders in the Jerusalem church by doing one thing while pretending to do another. The Holy Spirit, however, revealed their deception to Peter and protected the church from their corrupting influence. What Satan meant for evil, the Holy Spirit turned to good. He used this incident to instill greater respect for God and His divine mission for the church.

The Spirit Provides Leaders for the Church Engaged in Mission

One essential need of any church is Spirit-empowered leaders, men and women who are committed to Christ and qualified to lead the church in fulfilling its global mission. These leaders need godly wisdom and clear focus. The Holy Spirit is ready to provide the church with these leaders. He will empower and enable them to lead the church in such a way that it may become a powerful witness for Christ. The early church's choice of seven men to serve as "deacons" is an excellent example of how the Spirit does this (Acts 6:1–7).

When the apostles in Jerusalem saw the need to increase the number of leaders in the church, they did not appoint just anyone to this position. They wisely guided the church in choosing seven men who were "known to be full of the Spirit and wisdom" (Acts 6:3). Because the church was experiencing repeated outpourings of the Holy Spirit, they had no difficulty in finding such men. In their midst were many who were full of the Spirit and able to fill the leadership needs of the church.

The apostles appointed seven Spirit-filled men to serve the church as "deacons." These men were first given the task of taking care of an important administrative need in the church. However, they did more than administration. As Spirit-empowered leaders, they also proclaimed the gospel to the lost. You can read the stories of two of these men, Stephen and Philip, in Acts 6–8.

At the same time, the apostles reconfirmed their commitment to stay focused on prayer and the proclamation of the Word (Acts 6:4). Because of this Spirit-directed decision, "the word of God spread [and] the number of disciples in Jerusalem increased rapidly" (6:7).

The Spirit Guides the Church in its Mission

The missionary Spirit of God has a perfect plan and strategy for the church. In Chapter 2, we learned that as the third person of the Trinity, the Holy Spirit possesses all the attributes of God. He is therefore omnipotent (all-powerful), omniscient (all-knowing), and omnipresent (everywhere-present). Consequently, the Spirit can do all things, and He knows exactly what needs to be done to accomplish God's mission.

As we engage in evangelism, church planting, and missions, we can know that the Holy Spirit will guide every step of the way—if we will seek His face and listen to His voice.

Again, the book of Acts demonstrates this vital work of the Spirit. Through the guidance of the Spirit, the early church was amazingly successful in its mission efforts. Here are some examples:

- The Spirit guided Philip to the Ethiopian nobleman (Acts 8:29, 39).
- The Spirit guided Peter, and ultimately the whole church, into breaking past barriers of tradition to reach the Gentiles with the gospel (10:9–29).
- The Spirit guided Paul and his missionary team to Macedonia and Achaia where they successfully planted many churches (16:6–10).
- The Spirit compelled Paul to go to Jerusalem after his third missionary journey (20:22–23).

We conclude that the leadership and guidance of the Holy Spirit is a vital key to the church effectively fulfilling its mission.

THE APOSTOLIC MODEL: SPIRIT-EMPOWERED MINISTRY

Our study of the work of the Spirit in the ministry of the early church has valuable lessons for the church today. A truly biblical strategy for ministry and missions must look to the model found in the early church and in the ministry of the apostles. This apostolic model has at least three components: (1) Spirit empowerment, (2) missional commitment, and (3) bold witness. Let us now look at each of these components.

Spirit Empowerment

First, a truly apostolic model of ministry will contend for the absolute necessity of Spirit empowerment. This apostolic model affirms and promotes the following concepts:

- The empowerment of the Spirit is vitally important for all believers.
- The purpose of this divine empowering is to enable the church to proclaim the gospel and to advance Christ's mission to the ends of the earth.
- The empowerment of the Spirit is received through the experience of the baptism in the Holy Spirit.

The apostles did not deviate from their focus on Spirit empowerment. In addition to the examples in the book of Acts, Paul often referred in his epistles to the critical role of Spirit empowerment in his missionary work (Romans 15:18–21; 1 Corinthians 2:1–5; Colossians 1:29; 1 Thessalonians 1:5–8). The apostles knew this was an essential preparation for missional witness. They understood that first they needed to be empowered by the Spirit. They further understood that wherever they preached the gospel and planted the church, the believers in those churches must also be empowered by the Spirit. This empowering would equip them to participate as effective witnesses and church planters.

One example of the apostles' emphasis on Spirit empowerment is the account in Acts 8 of the church plant in Samaria. When the apostles in Jerusalem heard of the new church plant in Samaria, they immediately sent Peter and John to Samaria to pray for the Samaritan believers "that they might receive the Holy Spirit" (8:15). The apostles knew that for the gospel to spread from Samaria to other places, the believers in the new church needed to be empowered by the Spirit.

Another clear example of the apostolic emphasis on Spirit empowerment is Paul's ministry in Ephesus in Acts 19. When the apostle arrived in Ephesus, he found twelve disciples. His immediately asked them, "Did you receive the Holy Spirit when you believed?" (19:2). Paul had come to Ephesus to establish a church that would be a mission base from where he would reach all of Asia Minor (19:10). Paul asked the twelve men if they had received the Holy Spirit so that he could find out if they were ready to join him in that mission. When they answered "No," Paul immediately prayed for them, and "the Holy Spirit came on them, and they spoke in tongues and prophesied" (19:6).

Throughout his ministry, Paul never deviated from emphasizing the importance of believers being filled with the Spirit. Years later, Paul wrote back to this same church in Ephesus and urged them to continue seeking to be filled with the Spirit (Ephesians 5:18).

Missional Commitment

Not only will a truly apostolic model of ministry contend for the absolute necessity of Spirit empowerment, it will also demonstrate an

Chapter 7 ~ The Missionary Spirit in the Church

unwavering commitment to Christ's Great Commission (Matthew 28:18–20; Mark 16:15–18; Luke 24:45–49; John 20:21–22; Acts 1:4–5, 8).

The New Testament, and especially the book of Acts, tells how the early church sacrificially committed themselves to this task. The apostles believed that God's mission to redeem a people for himself from all nations was also their mission. This was why Jesus came, and it was the church's reason for being. God poured out the Holy Spirit on the church to equip the believers to fulfill that mission. Because of what Christ and the Holy Spirit had done in their lives, the apostles (and every member of the early church) wholeheartedly embraced Christ's mission as their own.

Bold Witness

Finally, a truly apostolic model of ministry will include bold, Spirit-empowered witness. This Spirit-empowered witness will be in two forms: Spirit-empowered *proclamation* of the gospel and Spirit-empowered *demonstration* of God's power to save, heal, and deliver. Let us look at each of those forms of witness.

Proclamation

The Spirit inspired the apostles to proclaim the message of salvation in Christ. Through repentance and faith in Jesus, people could be reconciled to God. The book of Acts contains several sermons preached by the apostles. A comparison of these messages reveals that they all focus on the person of Jesus. They explain His saving work and the need of all people to repent, believe, and follow Him.[25] The Holy Spirit kept the church focused on this message. It is the only message that will take people to heaven (Acts 4:12). This priority motivated Paul to remind the church in Corinth, "I resolved to

---

[25] Peter: Acts 2:14–40; 3:12–26; 4:8–12; 5:29–32; 10:34–43; Paul: Acts 13:16–41; 17:22–31; 22:1–21.

know nothing while I was with you except Jesus Christ and him crucified" (1 Corinthians 2:2). Any church that is truly full of the Holy Spirit will, like the apostolic church, never deviate from the central message of Christ.

Demonstration

The apostles not only proclaimed God's power to save, they also demonstrated His power through miraculous signs and wonders. The power of the Spirit enabled them to heal the sick, cast out demons, and perform miraculous signs. These miracles proved that the gospel is true and demonstrated that the kingdom of God had come in power.

The book of Acts highlights how miracles accompanied the proclamation of the gospel. When people saw the demonstration of God's power, they opened their hearts to the gospel and many turned to Christ.[26] Such demonstrations of the power of God were a prominent part of the apostolic witness. In a letter to the Christians in Thessalonica, Paul reminded them, "Our gospel came to you not simply with words but also with power, with the Holy Spirit and deep conviction" (1 Thessalonians 1:5).

Miracles performed in the power of the Holy Spirit contributed greatly to the missionary success of the apostles as they moved into new areas for evangelism and church planting. Any church today that claims to be full of the Spirit should boldly proclaim Christ and then expect the Holy Spirit to validate the preaching of the Word with miraculous signs.

IMPLICATIONS AND APPLICATIONS

The presence and power of the Spirit was the key to the early church's amazing missionary success. They received the power of the

---

[26] See Acts 9:32–35 (Aeneas); 9:36–42 (Dorcas); 13:6–12 (Elymas).

Spirit by being baptized in the Holy Spirit according to Jesus' promise in Acts 1:4–8. Further, even after the Day of Pentecost, the church continued to experience outpourings of the Spirit. This is because they made it a priority to continually seek the empowerment of the Spirit through prayer and by emphasizing the importance of all believers being empowered by the Holy Spirit.

The church today must do the same. We must take seriously Jesus' command to be filled with the Spirit. We should view the story of how the apostolic church ministered in the power of the Spirit as a definitive model for how the church should minister today and until Jesus returns.

We also need to remind ourselves constantly of the missional purpose of the baptism in the Holy Spirit. We must never forget how in Acts 1:8, Jesus connected the power of the Spirit to His mission. Sadly, many today have separated the promise of the Spirit's power from the mission. They seldom, if ever, challenge the church to commit itself to Christ's mission, nor do they emphasize the importance of being empowered by the Spirit to enable us for that mission. This must never be the case in our churches.

The power of the Holy Spirit is a prominent emphasis in many African churches. Tragically, however, the focus is often on personal miracles for believers rather than empowerment to reach the lost. Many Christians have become preoccupied with seeking God's blessings for themselves while ignoring God's purpose to bless the nations through the church. This is an unbiblical distortion of Jesus' final command and promise. Just as the Spirit powerfully enabled the early church to advance Christ's mission to the nations, He wants to empower the African church to do the same.

We must reconsecrate ourselves to the missional purpose of Pentecost. In doing this, we must also reconsecrate ourselves to Christ as our Lord and to obedience to the Great Commission. If we will humbly seek the power of God's Spirit and commit ourselves to be Christ's witnesses, He will pour out His Spirit on us. We should then engage in evangelism, church planting, and missions as never before. If we will follow the apostolic model for ministry, we can complete the mission of Christ in our generation. It is possible in the power of the Spirit

Questions for Discussion and Reflection.

1. What do you think is the most important element that the church needs to complete the great commission?

2. Why was it so important for the disciples to obey Jesus' final command? What are the missional implications of Jesus' final command for the church today?

3. Many people refer to the Day of Pentecost as the birthday of the church. Do you agree or disagree and why?

4. Is it possible for the church today to be as effective and successful in missions as the early church was? Explain your reasons.

5. How would you apply the apostolic model for ministry in your church?

~ CHAPTER 8 ~

THE MISSIONARY SPIRIT IN PERSONAL EXPERIENCE

In this section of the book, we have been discussing how the missionary Spirit is portrayed in the New Testament. We began in Chapter 6 by looking at how the missionary Spirit operated in the life and ministry of Jesus. Then in Chapter 7, we discussed the work of the missionary Spirit in the church. Now, in this final lesson of the section, we will investigate how God's missionary Spirit works in the personal experience of believers.

The transformation of sinners into saints is at the heart of God's mission and the Spirit's work. The Holy Spirit is God's agent who works to carry out God's redemptive mission. Every part of the Spirit's work in people is in some way connected to fulfilling that mission.

Repentant sinners come to know God only through the working of the Holy Spirit. Through His death and resurrection, Jesus prepared the way for salvation. Now, the Holy Spirit works to implement the redemption that Jesus made possible. Every part of the process of coming to faith and serving Christ and His mission is a work of the Spirit. In fact, without the work of the Spirit, it would be impossible for anyone to become a child of God and to live effectively for Him.

The Spirit works in people in numerous ways. In this chapter, we will examine these various works of the Spirit in the lives of individuals. We will do this by discussing the Spirit's work in three major categories:

- The Spirit regenerates sinners
- The Spirit sanctifies believers
- The Spirit enables workers

Each of these works of the Spirit is vital to the fulfillment of God's mission in the earth.

While the Spirit's work in people is presented throughout Scripture, it is especially evident in the New Testament. Further, in examining the work of the Holy Spirit in the New Testament, it is important to recognize the emphases of Paul in his letters and Luke in his Gospel and Acts. Paul deals more with the Spirit's work in regeneration and sanctification while Luke focuses primarily on the Spirit's work in empowering for witness.

THE SPIRIT REGENERATES SINNERS

The Spirit Prepares People for Salvation

Without Christ, every person is by nature a sinner and spiritually dead. They therefore live their lives according to the ways of the world and under the control of Satan (Ephesians 2:1–3). Unsaved people do not naturally understand nor accept the truth about God (Romans 8:5–8; 1 Corinthians 2:14). Satan has blinded them to the light of the gospel (2 Corinthians 4:4). They are unaware of their own spiritual need. Consequently, they need a miracle of grace to prepare them to receive the good news about Christ.

We find an example of this kind of miracle in Acts 16. Paul and his missionary team were speaking to a group of women in Philippi. As they spoke, the Holy Spirit worked in the heart of a woman named Lydia. The Scripture says, "The Lord opened her heart to respond to Paul's message" (16:14).

The missionary Spirit of God specializes in doing this marvelous work. He opens people's hearts and helps them see the truth of the gospel so that they might turn to Christ, put their faith in Him, and be saved.

Revealing Christ

The night before His crucifixion, Jesus told His disciples, "When the Helper comes…the Spirit of truth… He will testify about Me," (John 15:26, NASB). This declaration highlights the missionary nature of the Holy Spirit and His work. When a Spirit-filled believer shares the gospel with a lost sinner, the believer can be confident that the Holy Spirit is working in the sinner's heart to reveal Christ to that person. The Spirit is working to open the eyes of the spiritually blind sinner to enable them to understand the gospel and believe in Christ. This is why Paul could declare that God "made his light shine in our hearts to give us the light of the knowledge of God's glory displayed in the face of Christ" (2 Corinthians 4:6). God does this miraculous work by the "ministry of the Spirit" who works through those who proclaim the gospel (3:3, 6–8).

Convicting of Guilt

In conjunction with His work of revealing Christ to the lost, the Holy Spirit also works to "convict the world concerning sin and righteousness and judgment " (John 16:8, NASB). Take a moment now to read John 16:8–11. Notice how these verses teach some powerful truths about the Holy Spirit's missionary work of calling sinners to Christ. The Spirit's aim is to convince sinners of the evil of their sin and to persuade them to repent and turn in faith to Christ. This convicting work of the Holy Spirit is an essential step in preparing a sinner to receive Christ. Let us look at each of the three ways in which the Holy Spirit convicts sinners.

The Spirit convicts of sin. Jesus said that when the Holy Spirit comes, "he will convict the world concerning sin" (John 16:8, NASB). At its essence, sin is rebellion against God. It is the wellspring of all that is wrong in the world, and it is the reason humanity is lost and separated from God. Jesus went on to say that the Holy Spirit would convict the world of sin "because they do not believe in Me" (16:9). Here, He revealed the most serious of all sins—the refusal to believe in Christ. Jesus is the only way to salvation, and the Holy Spirit works to bring people to the point of acknowledging their sin and their need of the Savior.

The Spirit convicts concerning righteousness. Jesus also said that the Holy Spirit would "convict the world...concerning righteousness" (John 16:8, NASB). Righteousness is a fundamental characteristic of God's nature. His perfect righteousness stands in stark contrast to the sinful condition of humanity. The Jewish religious leaders thought Jesus was unrighteous, so they had Him crucified. However, His resurrection from the grave proved that He was truly God's righteous Servant (John 16:10; compare Acts 3:13–15). Further, through His death, resurrection, and ascension into heaven, Jesus made the way for repentant sinners to share in the righteousness of God (Romans 3:21–22; 2 Corinthians 5:21). The Holy Spirit works to convince lost sinners that faith in Christ is the only way they can be made righteous and be reconciled to God.

The Spirit convicts concerning judgment. Finally, Jesus said that when the Holy Spirit comes, He would "convict the world...concerning judgment" (John 16:8, NASB). The judgment of God is sure. Scripture affirms that God is the Righteous Judge who will one day judge the entire world (Matthew 12:36–37; Romans 2:5–6; Hebrews 9:27–28). When Christ rose from the dead, He defeated "the prince of this world," Satan (John 16:11). He sealed Satan's ultimate destiny. When Christ returns, God will put into effect His judgment against Satan. At that time, all who stand with Satan by refusing to follow Christ will be judged with him (Revelation 20:10–15). Many people do not believe this will happen (2 Peter 3:4). However, the Holy Spirit continues to work to convince them that God's judgment is real and that everyone who rejects Christ will someday stand before the judgment throne of God.

Drawing to Christ

Jesus declared, "No one can come to me unless the Father who sent me draws them" (John 6:44). The Father accomplishes His work of drawing unbelievers to Christ through the Holy Spirit. The Spirit works in them to reveal Christ and to provoke conviction in their hearts.

In most cases, the Spirit works through the anointed proclamation of the gospel message (Romans 10:12–15; compare 15:17–19). Since the Holy Spirit is a missionary Spirit, believers should always be sensitive to Him. They should allow Him to work in them and through them to draw unbelievers to Christ. The use of spiritual gifts, such as inspired prophetic messages, is one way the Spirit may draw people to Christ. Paul urged the church in Corinth to allow the Spirit to use them in the gift of prophecy so that unbelievers might be drawn to God (1 Corinthians 14:24–25).

The Spirit Saves and Transforms

The Spirit not only prepares people to respond to Christ in faith, but He also actively participates in their salvation experience. Paul wrote, "For by one Spirit we were all baptized into one body" (1 Corinthians 12:13, NASB). This means that when people commit their life to Christ, the Holy Spirit takes them and immerses them into the body of Christ. They are thus united with Christ and with other believers in Him.

To truly appreciate what the Bible teaches about salvation, we must understand that the New Testament presents salvation as both an objective fact and a transformational experience. The objective fact is Christ's finished work on the cross and our faith in that work. The transformational experience is the regenerative work of the Holy Spirit that occurs in our lives when we are born again (John 3:3–7; 2 Corinthians 5:17). Let us look more closely at each of these aspects of salvation.

Salvation: An Objective Fact

Through His death and resurrection, Christ made it possible for all people to receive forgiveness of their sins. This salvation changes a person's position in God and their relationship to Him. Here are some terms that describe the objective nature of a Christian's relationship to God:

Reconciliation. Through sinful rebellion, we were all alienated from God. However, He took the initiative by giving His Son to die in our place on the cross (John 3:16). He made the way for us to be reconciled with God through repentance and faith (Romans 5:9–11; 2 Corinthians 5:17–21).

Redemption. In addition to being separated from God, we were also enslaved in bondage to sin (John 8:34; Romans 6:6; 7:14). However, with His blood, Christ paid the required ransom to free us from sin's prison (Ephesians 1:7; 1 Peter 1:18–19; Revelation 5:9). Now, because Christ has paid the price for our redemption, we belong to God (1 Corinthians 6:20; 7:23).

Justification. We are all guilty of sin (Romans 3:23). We all deserve to be judged and condemned (2:5–8). However, by dying in our place on the cross, Christ made the way for us to be justified, or declared innocent and righteous before God (3:24).

Adoption. When we are saved, God adopts us into His family. We become children of God and brothers and sisters in Christ (Galatians 4:5; Ephesians 1:5).

Regeneration: An Internal Transformation

Salvation, however, is more than just an objective fact. It is also a transformational experience of new life in Christ. When a person is saved, the Holy Spirit imparts God's life to that individual and transforms them from the inside out. The closely related New Testament concepts of *regeneration* (or *rebirth*), *new birth,* and *renewal* help us understand the internal transforming work of the Holy Spirit.

Jesus explained to Nicodemus that faith in Christ results in a person's being *born again* by the Spirit of God (John 3:3–8). Because all humans are by nature "dead in [their] trespasses and sins," all need spiritual rebirth (Ephesians 2:1–5). This experience of rebirth and new life in Christ is known as regeneration and is accomplished by the Holy Spirit (2 Corinthians 5:17). Through new birth we truly become God's children (John 1:12–13). While all people are God's creatures, only those who have been born again by the Spirit and are led by the Spirit are the true sons and daughters of God (Romans 8:14-16).

The Bible also describes the work of the Spirit as a work of regeneration and renewal. Paul explained to Titus that God saves us "through the washing of regeneration and renewing by the Holy Spirit" (Titus 3:5, NASB).[27] Notice how Paul used the words

---

[27] The Greek word for "regeneration" is *paliggenesia.* It is found in two places in the New Testament (Matt. 19:28; Tit. 3:5). It suggests a state of complete change or renewal. Some Bible versions translates it as "rebirth" (NIV) or "new birth" (NLT).

regeneration and *renewing* synonymously to describe the transformation that the Spirit works in people when He washes them clean from sin and imparts the life of God to them. The Holy Spirit, who is the "Spirit of life," imparts God's life and makes everything new again (Romans 8:2). Paul affirmed, "Therefore, if anyone is in Christ, the new creation has come: The old has gone, the new is here!" (2 Corinthians 5:17). Through the regenerating and renewing work of the Spirit, people who were once spiritually dead are made alive in Christ (Ephesians 2:5; Colossians 2:13).

When a person is born again by the Spirit, there should be a noticeable change in his or her life. The old life of sin and rebellion against God has been transformed by the Spirit into a new life of righteousness and service to God (Ephesians 4:17–24). This transformation comes about as the person walks in the Spirit and follows His leading (Galatians 5:22–25). We will examine this more later in the chapter when we discuss the work of the Spirit in sanctification.

The Spirit Indwells and Gives Assurance of Salvation

The Spirit Indwells Believers

When someone receives Christ as Savior, the Holy Spirit enters and *indwells* that person (Galatians 4.6). He takes up residence in the new believer and begins to work in his or her life (Romans 8:9–12). In this way, by His indwelling presence, the Spirit imparts God's eternal life to that person. This indwelling presence of the Spirit is so essential to salvation that Paul declares, "If anyone does not have the Spirit of Christ, they do not belong to Christ" (Romans 8:9). New life in Christ is fully dependent on the indwelling of the Holy Spirit.

Chapter 8 ~ The Missionary Spirit in Personal Experience

The Spirit Gives Assurance of Salvation

When the Spirit enters a new believer's life, He gives that person an inner assurance that he or she is truly a child of God. Paul explained, "The Spirit himself testifies with our spirit that we are God's children" (Romans 8:16). In another place Paul wrote, "God's love has been poured out into our hearts through the Holy Spirit, who has been given to us" (Romans 5:5).

What an encouragement it is when the Spirit gives us assurance of God's amazing love and acceptance. Jesus promised that He would not leave us as orphans but would come to us (John 14:18). He fulfills this promise by sending His Holy Spirit to bear witness in our hearts that we are not alone—we are God's dearly loved children.

Indwelling Versus Empowerment

The indwelling work of the Spirit does not end with transformation and assurance. As we will discuss later in this chapter, the Spirit also sanctifies believers, enabling them to live holy lives (2 Thessalonians 2:13; 1 Peter 1:2). Further, He empowers them, enabling them to be effective witnesses for Christ (Luke 24:48–49; Acts 1:8). Every follower of Jesus must personally experience these important works of the Spirit if they are to fulfill God's plan for their lives.

The experience of being filled with (and thus empowered by) the Holy Spirit is a distinct work of the Spirit. We must not confuse it with being indwelt by the Spirit. As we have already seen, the Spirit indwells the new believer at salvation and continues to indwell every born-again believer. From the moment of conversion, the indwelling Spirit becomes the new believer's source of divine eternal life.

The empowerment of the Spirit for service is a further work of the Spirit. This grace is received when a person is baptized in the Holy Spirit. At that moment, the believer is enabled to fully participate in God's mission by being filled with and empowered by the Holy Spirit

(Acts 1:4–5, 8). We will briefly examine the empowering work of the Holy Spirit later in this chapter, but we will look at it in greater depth in the next section.

THE SPIRIT SANCTIFIES BELIEVERS

Sanctification is a second major work of God's missionary Spirit in the lives of believers. God requires that His people, who represent Him to a lost world, be sanctified and live holy lives (1 Thessalonians 4:3). This aspect of Christian living is so important that the Bible commands, "Make every effort to live in peace with everyone and to be holy; without holiness no one will see the Lord" (Hebrews 12:14). God's mission is to call people out of the world and prepare them for himself. As God's missionary people, the Spirit works in our hearts to transform us into Christ's image (2 Corinthians 3:18). We are to reflect His character, and we are to be holy because He is holy.

The story of the Bible demonstrates that it is impossible for us to achieve holiness on our own. Thankfully, however, the Holy Spirit is at work in our lives to enable us to become God's sanctified people, set apart by Him to fulfill His mission in the earth. Paul encouraged the Thessalonian church when he wrote that from the beginning, "God chose you…to be saved through the sanctifying work of the Spirit and through belief in the truth" (2 Thessalonians 2:13). God has not left us alone to achieve holiness by our own efforts. Let us now look at what holiness means and how the Spirit helps us live holy lives.

The Meaning of Sanctification

In the New Testament, the words *sanctification* and *holiness* are often used interchangeably. Therefore, as you read this chapter, be aware that both words are talking about the same thing. The Bible declares that God is holy; therefore, His people must also be holy (Leviticus 11:44–45; 19:2; 20:7, 26; 1 Peter 1:15). When we say God is holy, we mean that He is perfect, pure, and totally separate from everything that is evil.

Set Apart for God

To be sanctified means to be set apart from evil and dedicated to serve God alone. In the Old Testament, objects, places, and people were called holy because they had been set apart and dedicated to God's service. In the New Testament, for God's people to be sanctified, it meant they had been set apart from everything unholy, impure, and evil. It further meant that they were to be consecrated fully to God and dedicated to serving Him and His mission in the earth.

In his second letter to the church in Corinth, Paul presented this idea of being separated from evil and dedicated to God. He began by combining and quoting various Old Testament verses: "Therefore, 'Come out from them and be separate, says the Lord. Touch no unclean thing, and I will receive you.' And, 'I will be a Father to you, and you will be my sons and daughters, says the Lord Almighty'" (2 Corinthians 6:17–18). Then, based on this promise of God to accept His people if they will separate themselves from impurity, Paul made the following conclusion: "Since we have these promises, dear friends, let us purify ourselves from everything that contaminates body and spirit, perfecting holiness out of reverence for God" (2 Corinthians 7:1).

The Time of Sanctification

Some Scripture passages talk about sanctification as something that has already been achieved in the believer's life. Other passages talk about sanctification as a goal that believers should strive to achieve. In this way, the New Testament presents sanctification as both a completed work of grace in the believer and an ongoing process in the believer's Christian walk.

Chapter 8 ~ The Missionary Spirit in Personal Experience

Sanctification Is Immediate

The immediate nature of sanctification is demonstrated by the fact that in the New Testament, Christians are often called "saints." The word *saints* literally means "holy ones." When a person puts his or her faith in Christ, they are immediately sanctified and made holy by a work of God's grace. For example, Paul wrote, "To the church of God in Corinth, to those sanctified in Christ Jesus and called to be his holy people" (1 Corinthians 1:2). This does not mean that these early Christians were perfect. In fact, the rest of 1 Corinthians shows that they were struggling with a number of sinful attitudes and practices. Nevertheless, the fact that Paul referred to these believers as "sanctified" and "holy people" indicates that they truly belonged to God. He had set them apart to live in dedicated service to Him. So in this sense, sanctification occurs instantaneously when a person is saved.

Sanctification Is Ongoing

Other Scripture passages indicate that sanctification is an ongoing process. It is ongoing in the sense that every Christian must daily live out the kind of holy, consecrated life that God requires. This can only be done as believers walk in the Spirit, allowing Him to continually renew and transform their lives. The following texts show that sanctification needs to be continually perfected, completed, and pursued:

- "Therefore, since we have these promises, dear friends, let us purify ourselves from everything that contaminates body and spirit, *perfecting holiness* out of reverence for God" (2 Corinthians 7:1, emphasis added).
- "May God himself, the God of peace, *sanctify you through and through.* May your whole spirit, soul and body be kept

blameless at the coming of our Lord Jesus Christ" (1 Thessalonians 5:23, emphasis added),

- "*Make every effort* to live in peace with everyone and *to be holy*; without holiness no one will see the Lord" (Hebrews 12:14, emphasis added).

The Key to Sanctification

Live by the Spirit

When we are born again, we come into a living relationship with Christ through the Holy Spirit who dwells in us. However, that is only the beginning of the Spirit's work in our lives. Because of our sinful nature, we need the Holy Spirit to enable us to live according to God's holy requirements each day. An ongoing relationship with the Spirit of God is essential to living the sanctified life. Christ died for us to set us free from the penalty of sin. Now, the Holy Spirit lives in us to set us free from the controlling power of sin.

The Bible teaches that there are two ways we may choose to live our lives. The first way is what Paul referred to as living "according to the flesh" (Romans 8:4–8, 12–13). To live according to the flesh is to live apart from God and according to the desires of the sinful nature. It is to live with our minds set on the sinful desires of the flesh (8:5). Scripture warns us that living in this way leads to death (Romans 8:13; Galatians 6:8).

Thankfully, there is an alternate way to live. Paul called it living "according to the Spirit" (Romans 8:4–5). The person who lives according to the Spirit lives according to the desire and will of the Holy Spirit (Romans 8:5–6; Galatians 5:16–17).

Scripture promises that if we will walk in the power of the Holy Spirit, He will enable us to live holy lives. Paul wrote, "If by the Spirit you put to death the misdeeds of the body, you will live" (Romans 8:13). Submitting to the leading of the Spirit and walking in His power is the key to overcoming temptation and living above our sinful desires. Paul affirmed this truth when he declared, "Walk in the Spirit, and you will not gratify the desires of the flesh" (Galatians 5:16). As we walk in the Spirit, we align our desires with His. The Spirit then empowers us to overcome our evil desires and to walk in righteousness.

Be Filled with the Spirit

To walk by the Spirit, one must first be filled with the Spirit (Ephesians 5:18). Jesus referred to the initial experience of being filled with the Spirit as being "baptized in the Holy Spirit" (Acts 1:5, compare 2:4). In the next section, we will examine this experience in greater detail, especially as it relates to empowerment for witness. For now, however, it is essential that we understand that before a person can live by the Spirit, he or she must be filled with the Spirit and must remain full of the Spirit.

Paul emphasized the importance of being filled with the Spirit in order to live a sanctified life. He urged the Ephesians: "Do not be foolish, but understand what the Lord's will is. Do not get drunk on wine, which leads to debauchery. *Instead, be filled with the Spirit"* (Ephesians 5:17–18, emphasis added).

Those who accept Christ but then fail to walk in the Spirit easily fall prey to sinful desires and old habits. As long as we live in our earthly bodies, the sinful nature will be present and active. The only way to overcome the sinful nature is by being filled with the Spirit and then walking continually in the Spirit's power. After salvation, the most important step for every believer is to be filled with the Spirit.

The Results of Sanctification

Christlike Character

The goal of the Spirit's work in sanctification is to make us more like Christ and to enable us to represent Him better to a dying world. Paul declared, "Those God foreknew he also predestined to be conformed to the image of his Son" (Romans 8:29). When we are filled with the Holy Spirit and daily submit to His work in us, He enables us to follow Christ's example and live holy lives—lives that glorify God.

Spiritual Fruit

As the Spirit transforms us to be more like Christ, evidence of this transformation will appear. The Bible calls this evidence "the fruit of the Spirit." The fruit of the Spirit is simply the character of Christ that the Spirit produces in us as we live by the Spirit's power. In Galatians 5, Paul provides a list of the kind of fruit the Spirit will produce as we live under His control: "The fruit of the Spirit is love, joy, peace, patience, kindness, goodness, faithfulness, gentleness, self-control" (Galatians 5:22–23, NASB).

Paul ends his list of spiritual fruit with the affirmation, "Against *such things* there is no law" (Galatians 5:23, emphasis added). This statement suggests that this list is representative of the kind of fruit the Spirit works to produce in our lives. The Spirit also strives to produce other godly characteristics in our lives such as humility, self-sacrifice, perseverance, and generosity. Peter gives us a list that is similar to Paul's: "Make every effort to add to your faith, goodness; and to goodness, knowledge; and to knowledge, self-control; and to self-control, perseverance; and to perseverance, godliness; and to godliness, mutual affection; and to mutual affection, love" (2 Peter 1:5–7). Christ exhibited all these qualities as He walked here on earth.

In fact, every godly quality found in Christ could be included in the list of fruit the Spirit desires to produce in us.

Growing in Christlikeness is not optional for Christians. Jesus warned, "[My Father] cuts off every branch in me that bears no fruit, while every branch that does bear fruit he prunes so that it will be even more fruitful" (John 15:2). Every follower of Christ bears the responsibility to walk in the Spirit each day and allow Him to produce fruit in their life.

Sometimes Pentecostal Christians mistakenly value the more spectacular gifts of the Spirit over the less spectacular fruit of the Spirit. This error can lead to an unbiblical and dangerous imbalance in those who seek miracles but refuse to surrender themselves to the sanctifying work of the Spirit. Jesus sternly warned about such misguided attitudes in His Sermon on the Mount (Matthew 7:15–23).

The Spirit's work in both miraculous gifts and sanctifying believers is vital to fulfilling God's mission. He wants to draw the world to himself through both the testimony of His mighty works and the Christlike lives of His people. Both are necessary, and both should be highly valued.

Witness

The fruit of the Spirit also play an essential role in fulfilling the *missio Dei.* Our exemplary, Christlike lives are a vital part of our witness to the world. Jesus has commanded us, "Let your light shine before others, that they may see your good deeds and glorify your Father in heaven" (Matthew 5:16). The Holy Spirit plays a major role in this process. Paul wrote, "God's love has been poured out into our hearts through the Holy Spirit, who has been given to us" (Romans 5:5). The Spirit works to fill our hearts with Christ's love for the world.

It is not coincidental that love is the first fruit of the Spirit mentioned in Paul's list in Galatians 5:22–23. Christ loves the Father, and He loves the church. He also loves those who are lost in sin. Because of His great love for lost humanity, Christ gave His life in service to the Father's mission. He did this to save the world. When we walk in the Spirit and allow the Holy Spirit to produce His fruit in our lives, we too will love our Heavenly Father. We will also love Christ and those for whom He died. This love will prompt us to respond to the Father by participating in His mission to save the nations.

A well-known adage states, "Actions speak louder than words." This is true! And this truth makes us realize the importance of living God-honoring lives. Being a witness for Christ involves the way we live. When we display the fruit of the Spirit, we please God and glorify Him. We become living testimonies to the world that Christ has truly transformed us and can do the same for others.

THE SPIRIT ENABLES WORKERS

A third major category of the missionary work of the Spirit is His work of enabling believers for effective service to God. Every believer has an important role to play in God's mission, and the Holy Spirit's power is the key that enables believers to fulfill their part in that mission.

In Chapter 2, we learned that *Paraclete* is one of the names for the Holy Spirit. This Greek word can mean Helper, Counselor, or Advocate. Jesus himself was a Paraclete who helped His disciples while He was here on earth. Today, He continues to help us as our Heavenly Intercessor (Hebrews 7:25; 1 John 2:1).

As Jesus was preparing to return to heaven, He promised to send the Holy Spirit who would come to help us as another Paraclete. Jesus further promised that the Holy Spirit would remain with us forever (John 14:15). Jesus explained that the Holy Spirit, in His role as our Paraclete, would teach us, guide us, and enable us to serve God and carry out His mission.

God is sovereign. He could have chosen another way to accomplish His mission. However, He sovereignly chose to work by His Spirit through His people to call the nations to himself. What a privilege God has granted us to participate in His mission. It is the most important work in all the world.

Now we will examine some of the ways the Spirit works through us, enabling us to advance God's mission.

The Spirit Empowers Us

A primary role of the Spirit is to help Jesus' followers effectively participate in God's mission as His witnesses. The Spirit sovereignly bears witness to Christ (John 15:26). He works to "convict the world concerning sin and righteousness and judgment" (16:7–8, NASB). He also gives power to Christ's followers to enable them to join in the mission by continuing the work that Jesus began (Acts 1:8).

On the eve of His crucifixion, Jesus talked to His disciples about the coming of the Holy Spirit. He declared, "Whoever believes in me will do the works I have been doing, and they will do even greater things than these, because I am going to the Father" (John 14:12). The works of Jesus included His powerful teaching and preaching along with the many miracles He performed. By observing these powerful works and hearing His powerful message, many were moved to put their faith in Christ and be saved. These followers of Christ constituted the beginning of the church.

Jesus did not accomplish the powerful works that He did (and which He said His followers would continue to do) in human strength. According to Jesus, He carried out His work through the anointing of the Holy Spirit that rested on His life (Luke 4:18–19). Today, His followers must do the same (Acts 1:4–5, 8).

After declaring that His followers would continue His work, Jesus explained that this would only be possible because He would send them the same Holy Spirit who had enabled Him. "I will ask the

Father," He promised, "and He will give you another Helper, that He may be with you forever" (John 14:16, NASB; compare 16:7–8).

When the Holy Spirit comes on and fills believers, He empowers them to participate in God's mission. He enables them to proclaim the gospel powerfully and to serve Christ effectively in establishing His church around the world. Jesus emphasized this mission in His last words before He ascended into heaven. He declared, "You will receive power when the Holy Spirit comes on you; and you will be my witnesses…to the ends of the earth" (Acts 1:8).

In addition, the Spirit gives various ministry and spiritual gifts to enable the church to fulfill its mission. We will examine these gifts in more detail in the next section. We will also examine what the New Testament teaches concerning the baptism in the Holy Spirit and Spirit-empowered ministry.

The Spirit Teaches Us

Another significant way the Holy Spirit helps us advance God's mission is by teaching us. Jesus promised, "But the Helper, the Holy Spirit, whom the Father will send in My name, He will teach you all things, and bring to your remembrance all that I said to you." (John 14:26, NASB).

As the first disciples followed Jesus, they listened to His teaching. After Jesus went back to heaven, He sent the Holy Spirit to continue to teach them. They were filled with the Spirit and followed the Spirit's leading. As they did, He gave them greater understanding concerning Christ's words and mission. This is what happened to Peter in Acts 10 in the story of the outpouring of the Spirit on the household of Cornelius. The Holy Spirit helped Peter understand that salvation is truly for all people from every nation (Acts 10:34–35). The Spirit also helped the apostles remember and accurately record what Jesus had taught them. Because of this, we can be assured that what we have recorded in the Gospels accurately communicates what Jesus said and meant.

Today, the Holy Spirit continues His teaching ministry. As we studied in Chapter 3, when we study the Bible with our hearts open to God, the Spirit will come and illuminate our understanding of God's Word. Without the Spirit's guidance, we would surely fall into the trap of error and false doctrine. Paul urged Timothy to guard the sound teaching of the gospel with the help of the Holy Spirit who dwelt in him (2 Timothy 1:13–14). The Spirit will do the same for us today if we will submit ourselves to Him and seek His guidance. Further, in our daily lives and ministries, He will bring to mind passages of Scripture that we have hidden in our hearts to encourage and strengthen us.

The Spirit Guides Us

Another way the Holy Spirit helps in fulfilling God's mission is by guiding us. Throughout the book of Acts, we observe the Spirit of God guiding Christ's followers as they went about preaching the gospel. For instance, in Acts 8, the Spirit guided Philip to the Ethiopian nobleman (8:26–29). Then in Acts 15, He guided the church in making important decisions that would profoundly affect the future mission of the church (15:28). Again, in Acts 16, during Paul's second missionary journey, the Spirit guided the apostle and his missionary team to Macedonia to preach the gospel there (16:6–10). These are but three of the many examples of how the Holy Spirit guided the work in Acts.

The Spirit knows all things, and He knows best where we should go and what we should do to advance God's mission. We should trust the Spirit and seek His guidance. Jesus promised, "When he, the Spirit of truth, comes, he will guide you into all truth" (John 16:13). As we daily seek to be filled with His presence and ask for His guidance, we can be assured that the Holy Spirit will direct our paths.

The Spirit Helps Us Pray

The Holy Spirit also enables us to advance God's mission by helping us pray. Through prayer, we draw near to God, speak to Him, and hear His voice when He speaks. In addition, through intercessory prayer, we partner with God to see people set free from satanic bondage. As Spirit-filled disciples competently wield the weapon of prayer, the church boldly advances against the kingdom of darkness (Ephesians 6:12, 18). God's Word confirms what God's people have learned from experience: on our own, we are weak and incompetent. In the words of Paul, "We do not know what we ought to pray for" (Romans 8:26).

Thankfully, however, in such situations the Spirit will come to our aid. He knows God's will perfectly, and He stands ready to help us pray in accordance with God's will (Romans 8:27). He does this by interceding through us "with groaning too deep for words" (8:26). In the New Testament, this practice is sometimes described as "praying in the Spirit" (Ephesians 6:18; Jude 20; compare 1 Corinthians 14:14–15). As we intercede in the Spirit, we are not on our own. The Holy Spirit prays through us, enabling us to pray by His power. When our own attempts at prayer fail, the Spirit takes over and prays through us, and He prays powerfully in accordance with the will of God. Prayer in tongues is a major way we pray in the Spirit. To pray in the Spirit, one must be filled with the Spirit.

The Spirit Strengthens Us

A final way the Spirit enables us to advance God's mission in the earth is by strengthening us during times of persecution and trial. Jesus taught that following Him would not always be easy. He reminded His followers, "In this world you will have trouble" (John 16:33). He further warned that those who seek to advance His kingdom would face persecution (Matthew 24:9; Luke 21:12; John 15:20). The apostle Paul affirmed the same in his letters (1

Thessalonians 3:4; 2 Timothy 3:12; compare Acts 14:22). We should not be surprised when persecution comes our way.

However, Jesus also gave an encouraging promise. He said that the Holy Spirit would come and provide strength and wisdom, enabling us to remain true to Christ and to continue to advance His mission in times of persecution. In each of the Synoptic Gospels, Jesus told His disciples not to worry about what to say or how to defend themselves if they were arrested for preaching the gospel. He promised, "The Holy Spirit will teach you at that time what you should say" (Luke 12:12; compare Matthew 10:19–20; Mark 13:11).

This promise of Jesus is fulfilled many times in the book of Acts. Just before he was stoned to death, Stephen was filled with the Holy Spirit and spoke courageously on Christ's behalf (Acts 6:12–7:56; compare 6:15; 7:55). On another occasion, Peter was brought before the Jewish Sanhedrin. As He did with Stephen, the Spirit empowered Peter to speak boldly in the face of danger (Acts 4:8–12). This same pattern is repeated throughout the book of Acts. In each instance, the Holy Spirit gave Christ's witnesses courage and strength to persevere in the face of danger. Undaunted, they continued to move forward in obedience to their Savior's Great Commission.

The Holy Spirit will do the same for us today. No matter what difficulties we may face, the Spirit of Missions is ready to provide encouragement, wisdom, and strength for the challenge.

IMPLICATIONS AND APPLICATIONS

In this chapter, we have learned that the work of the Holy Spirit is indispensable to the Christian life. Our experience with the Spirit will impact every aspect of our walk with Christ—from salvation to sanctification to service for God. It follows then that every follower of Jesus must fully experience the Spirit's work in his or her life.

An effective Christian life is not possible without the powerful working of the Spirit. To live a life pleasing to God, and to bear effective witness for Him, every believer needs to be empowered by the Spirit. As soon as people come to faith in Christ, it is important that we teach them about the Holy Spirit. Upon being born again, they are indwelt by the Holy Spirit, and we should encourage them to also be baptized with the Spirit so that they can live and minister by the power of the Spirit.

We must also teach new believers about the mission of the Spirit and challenge them to accept their responsibility to join Him in His mission. Every child of God is required to follow the example of Christ and live a holy, dedicated life. We must teach every new believer to seek the Spirit's fullness and to live fully submitted to God's Word and God's Spirit. How foolish we would be to neglect the powerful work of the Spirit and not seek His presence and power in our lives.

Questions for Discussion and Reflection

1. How should an understanding of the essential role of the Holy Spirit in bringing people to Christ affect our preparation for and engagement in witnessing to the lost?

2. Does the Holy Spirit use people who have been regenerated but not baptized in the Holy Spirit? What difference is there for those who have been baptized in the Holy Spirit?

3. If people receive the indwelling of the Spirit at salvation, why is it still necessary for them to also be baptized in the Holy Spirit?

4. In light of the progressive work of sanctification, how important is teaching and preaching on the work of the Spirit in the church and why?

5. What is the relation between the baptism in the Holy Spirit and the five ways in which the Holy Spirit enables believers identified in this chapter?

Chapter 8 ~ The Missionary Spirit in Personal Experience

~ Part Four ~

Empowered by the Missionary Spirit

~ CHAPTER 9 ~

Baptism in the Holy Spirit: Its Missional Purpose

Completing God's mission to redeem lost people out of every tribe, language, and nation is the most important work on earth. It is so important that Jesus willingly suffered on the cross to make it possible. He now calls us, His church, to join Him in that mission. He commands us to "go into all the world and preach the gospel to all creation" and to "make disciples of all nations" (Mark 16:15; Matthew 28:19).

Left on our own, however, we would surely fail. We can accomplish God's mission only with God's help. Thankfully, He has promised to give us His power to enable us to do just that. We receive that power when we are baptized in the Holy Spirit.

With this lesson, we begin the final section of our study. In this section, we will examine the biblical experience known as the baptism in the Holy Spirit. We will discover how this powerful experience enables us to serve God more perfectly and to execute His mission more powerfully.

In this lesson, we will define the experience. We will then examine its missional purpose and nature. In the next lesson, we will look at two missional signs that always accompany Spirit baptism. Then, we will discuss how a person can personally receive the experience. Finally, in the concluding lesson of our study, we will discuss how a person can minister in the Spirit's power.

THE EXPERIENCE DEFINED

What exactly is this experience Scripture calls the baptism in the Holy Spirit? In Scripture the experience is described in several ways, including being baptized in the Holy Spirit, being filled with the Spirit, the Spirit coming (or falling) on believers, an outpouring, and a gift and promise from God. We will discuss each of these concepts later in this lesson.

The baptism in the Holy Spirit is a powerful, life-changing experience available to all Christians. It occurs when the Holy Spirit comes on a committed follower of Christ, filling, transforming, and empowering that person's life. Jesus identified the baptism in the Holy Spirit as an experience of divine power given by God to enable His people to effectively participate in His mission (Acts 1:8).

Throughout this study, we have emphasized that a clear understanding of God's mission is essential to a correct understanding of the work of the Holy Spirit. This fact is supremely true when it comes to understanding the baptism in the Holy Spirit. The baptism in the Holy Spirit is more than a doctrine to believe; it is an experience to embrace. It is not to be confused with the indwelling of the Spirit that we receive when we are born again. Spirit baptism is a separate life-transforming encounter with the power and presence of the Holy Spirit.

Spirit baptism occurs when the Holy Spirit comes on a believer, to fill and empower that person for effective witness. This is what happened to the 120 disciples on the Day of Pentecost: "All of them were filled with the Holy Spirit and began to speak in other tongues as the Spirit enabled them" (Acts 2:4, compare 1:4). Spirit baptism is repeated in various contexts throughout the book of Acts (4:31; 8:16–17; 9:17–18; 10:44–46; 19:6).

ITS MISSIONAL PURPOSE

All four Gospels tell how John the Baptist announced that Jesus would baptize His followers in the Holy Spirit (Matthew 3:11; Mark 1:8; Luke 3:16; John 1:33). This suggests that the message of Spirit baptism was at the heart of gospel proclamation in the early church. These passages, however, do not explain the purpose of the experience. For that, we must look to the words of Jesus.

Jesus revealed the primary purpose of Spirit baptism in His last message before He ascended into heaven. He commanded the disciples: "Do not leave Jerusalem, but wait for the gift my Father promised, which you have heard me speak about. For John baptized with water, but in a few days you will be baptized with the Holy Spirit" (Acts 1:4–5). Jesus then told them why they would be baptized in the Holy Spirit. He said, "You will receive power when the Holy Spirit comes on you; and you will be my witnesses in Jerusalem, and in all Judea and Samaria, and to the ends of the earth" (1:8). The primary purpose of Spirit baptism is empowerment for missional witness.

The fact that this was Jesus' final directive to the church reveals the importance He placed on this experience. He wanted His disciples to make being empowered by the Holy Spirit a priority in their own lives and ministries. They were to be empowered by the Spirit before they began their ministries, and they were to teach their disciples to do the same.

In previous chapters, we discussed how the Holy Spirit works in people's lives in many wonderful ways. We must never forget, however, that Jesus consistently connected the experience of Spirit baptism to His redemptive mission. Through the baptism in the Holy Spirit, God transforms His missionary people into a powerful

Chapter 9 ~ Baptism in the Holy Spirit: Its Missional Purpose

missional force. The book of Acts demonstrates this missional purpose of Spirit baptism by citing multiple instances when God's Spirit came on and filled God's people. In each instance, the result was invariably the same—missional witness. Here are six of those instances:

- Acts 2:1–4 (Jerusalem, on the Day of Pentecost)
- Acts 4:31–33 (Jerusalem, following persecution)[28]
- Acts 8:14–20 (Samaria)
- Acts 9:17–18 (Damascus, Saul of Tarsus)
- Acts 10:44–47 (Caesarea)
- Acts 19:1–7 (Ephesus)

In each account, the Spirit's coming on believers resulted in empowered witness, which caused the church to grow and also expanded its missionary outreach.

These occurrences of Spirit baptism took place over an extended period of time. The final outpouring in Ephesus occurred some twenty-five years after the first outpouring at Pentecost. This fact demonstrates that God continued to pour out the Spirit on the church long after the Day of Pentecost. God still wants to pour out His Spirit on believers in the church today, enabling them to continue advancing His mission "to the ends of the earth" (Acts 1:8).

To better understand the experience of Spirit baptism, we must consider two important characteristics of this experience. First, the baptism in the Holy Spirit is an empowering experience that is distinct and separate from salvation. Second, it is a normative experience, meaning that it is intended for every Christian.

---

[28] In this instance, some, who had been baptized in the Spirit on the Day of Pentecost, were filled again with the Spirit, while others were filled for the first time.

A Distinct Empowering Experience

The baptism in the Holy Spirit is an experience that is separate and distinct from the new birth. It occurs subsequent to (after) salvation. While it is possible for someone to receive Christ as Savior and then immediately be baptized in the Holy Spirit (as is demonstrated by the outpouring of the Spirit in Caesarea in Acts 10), the most common pattern we see in Acts is a clear period of time between people being saved and being baptized in the Holy Spirit. These theological concepts are known as "subsequence" and "separability." Subsequence refers to the concept that Spirit baptism occurs after the new birth—if not always chronologically, at least logically and theologically. Separability refers to the concept that Spirit baptism is a spiritual experience distinct from the new birth.

The concepts of subsequence and separability are important because of the missional purpose and nature of the experience. Jesus does not baptize sinners in the Spirit to transform them into Christians; He baptizes Christians in the Holy Spirit to transform them into powerful witnesses. This truth is demonstrated in several accounts in Acts where Spirit baptism is clearly shown to be distinct from salvation. In each of these accounts, the context reveals the missional purpose of the experience. Let us look at some of these accounts in the book of Acts. As you begin each section, take time to read the verses indicated in the heading.

The 120 at Pentecost (Read Acts 2:1–4)

Those who gathered in Jerusalem to await the Spirit's outpouring were genuinely saved. As followers of Jesus Christ, they had put their faith in Him, repented of their sins, and committed themselves to serve their Lord (Luke 18:28). Some of them, like the apostles, had been following Jesus for several years.

Previously, Jesus had declared to His followers that they had been cleansed (John 13:10; 15:3) and that their names were written in heaven (Luke 10:20). He had further authorized and commissioned them to go and proclaim His name to the nations (Matthew 28:18–20). He had even breathed on them and told them to "receive the Holy Spirit" (John 20:22). Later, after Jesus ascended into heaven, these men and women obediently spent a week or more in constant worship and prayer awaiting the fulfillment of Christ's promise to pour out His Spirit on them (Luke 24:53; Acts 1:14).

These men and women were obviously a group of committed believers. Therefore, when they were baptized in the Holy Spirit on the Day of Pentecost, they were clearly not experiencing salvation for the first time or being initiated into God's kingdom. Rather, just as Jesus had promised in Acts 1:8, they were being empowered by the Spirit for the mission Christ had given them.

The Samaritan Believers (Read Acts 8:5–17)

The story of the conversion and subsequent empowering of the new believers in Samaria is possibly the clearest example in Acts of the distinction between the work of the Spirit in salvation and Spirit baptism. Philip was one of the seven Spirit-filled "deacons" chosen in Acts 6. When the Jerusalem Christians were scattered because of persecution, Philip went to Samaria. There, he proclaimed the gospel powerfully, accompanied by miraculous signs (Acts 8:4–7). Many "believed Philip as he proclaimed the good news of the kingdom of God and the name of Jesus Christ" and were saved (8:12). As a result, there was "great joy in that city" (8:8). After these Samaritans made the decision to embrace Christ, Philip baptized them in water (8:12). But still, "the Holy Spirit had not yet come on any of them; they had simply been baptized in the name of the Lord Jesus" (8:16). Several days passed before Peter and John came down from Jerusalem, laid hands on them, and "they received the Holy Spirit" (8:17).

Some people suggest that the Samaritans were not truly converted until Peter and John prayed for them and they received the Spirit.

However, this idea is wrong. One reason why we know that the Samaritans' conversion was genuine is because throughout Acts, any time someone believed the gospel message, as did the Samaritans, they were always regarded as being truly saved.[29] Furthermore Philip, a man "full of the Spirit and wisdom" (Acts 6:3–5), would never have baptized the Samaritans had they not been truly saved.

More importantly, the language Luke used to describe how the Samaritans would receive the Spirit indicates that it was to be a missionally empowering experience. Luke stated that "the Holy Spirit had not yet *come on* any of them" (Acts 8:16, emphasis added). The phrase "come on" echoes Jesus' promise in Acts 1:8: "You will receive power when the Holy Spirit *comes on* you; and you will be my witnesses in…*Samaria,* and to the ends of the earth." When the Holy Spirit came on the Samaritans, this was a fulfillment of Jesus' missional promise.

Like every other Christ-follower, the Samaritan Christians were called to join in the work of witnessing for the kingdom of God. To do so, they needed to be empowered by the Holy Spirit, and that is exactly what happened to them. As a result, "the church throughout Judea, Galilee *and Samaria*…was strengthened" and "it increased in numbers" (Acts 9:31, emphasis added).

Saul of Tarsus (Read Acts 9:1–22)

The story of Saul's conversion and subsequent filling with the Spirit is a third example of Spirit baptism as a missionally empowering experience distinct from salvation. Luke repeated the story three times in the book of Acts (9:1–8; 22:4–11; 26:12–18). Combining these three accounts gives us a complete picture of what happened.

---

[29] E.g. Acts 2:41; 4:4; 9:42; 10:43; 11:21; 13:12, 39, 48; 14:1; 16:31, 34; 17:12, 34; 18:8.

Chapter 9 ~ Baptism in the Holy Spirit: Its Missional Purpose

As Saul neared the city of Syrian Damascus, he encountered the risen Christ. Blinded by the Savior's radiance, Saul had to be led by the hand into the city. Three days later, the Lord sent a disciple named Ananias to pray with Saul. Ananias said to Saul, "The Lord—Jesus, who appeared to you on the road as you were coming here—has sent me so that you may see again and be filled with the Holy Spirit" (Acts 9:17). Saul needed to be filled with the Spirit because Jesus had commissioned him to take the gospel to the Gentiles (Acts 9:15; 22:15–18). It was not enough that Saul had received a vision of Jesus; He also needed to be empowered by the Holy Spirit to enable him to effectively fulfill his ministry.

As with the Samaritan converts, some people argue that Saul was not truly converted until Ananias laid hands on him and he was filled with the Spirit. However, for the following reasons it is clear that Saul was first converted on the road to Damascus and then filled with the Spirit three days later when Ananias prayed for him:

- Saul called Jesus "Lord" two times, once before and once after Jesus revealed himself to Saul (Acts 9:5; 22:8–10; compare Romans 10:9; 1 Corinthians 12:3).
- Saul immediately submitted himself to Jesus and asked Jesus to tell him what do (Acts 22:10).
- On the Damascus road Jesus commissioned Saul to be His witness (Acts 9:15; 26:16–18).
- Ananias called Saul "brother" when he prayed for him, indicating that he accepted Saul as a fellow Christian and no longer a persecutor (Acts 9:17; 22:13).

Luke provided no further details about what happened when Saul was filled with the Spirit. He expected his readers to know that Saul was filled with the Spirit since that was why the Lord sent Ananias to pray for him (Acts 9:17). Additionally, Luke stated, "At once [Saul] began to preach in the synagogues that Jesus is the Son of God"

(9:20). Saul's bold witness indicates that he had been empowered by the Spirit, just as Jesus promised in Acts 1:8. Much of the remainder of the book of Acts portrays Saul (who would later be called Paul) as a Spirit-empowered minister who proclaimed the gospel with great power (see Acts 13:1–2, 9–12; 19:6–8, 11–12).

The Household of Cornelius (Read Acts 10:1–11:17)

The fourth example of Spirit baptism in Acts occurred in the city of Caesarea. It involved a Roman centurion named Cornelius and his household. Cornelius was a God-fearing Gentile who had rejected paganism and had chosen to follow the God of Israel. The Holy Spirit sent Peter to Cornelius to proclaim the good news concerning Christ.

The story of Cornelius plays a special role in the book of Acts. The experience of this man and his household was instrumental in moving Jewish believers in the early church into a fuller engagement in God's mission to all people. It also showed the leaders of the Jerusalem church that God intended for Gentiles to participate in His mission. God wanted these leaders to understand that He wants every believer to be empowered by the Spirit and to join His mission of taking the good news to all nations.

Cornelius and his family likely believed Peter's message and received salvation as they listened to him preach. This is not surprising since they were all "devout and God-fearing" people (Acts 10:2). Then, "While Peter was still speaking these words, the Holy Spirit came on all who heard the message" (10:44), and the other believers with Peter heard them "speaking in tongues and praising God" (10:46). This is exactly what had happened to the disciples on the Day of Pentecost (Acts 2:4, 11). Because of this, Peter and his Jewish companions understood that God welcomed the Gentiles into His kingdom as full participants in His mission.

In every other instance of Spirit baptism in Acts, there was a clear separation of time between the people's experience of salvation and

Chapter 9 ~ Baptism in the Holy Spirit: Its Missional Purpose

their baptism in the Holy Spirit. In this one instance, however, God took the initiative and immediately poured out His Spirit on these new believers. Ideally, believers should be empowered with the Spirit immediately after believing in Christ for salvation.

There are at least three important missional reasons why God poured out His Spirit in this way on Cornelius and his household:

1. Gentiles can be saved. First, God wanted to show that Gentiles could be saved through faith in Christ alone without first converting to Judaism and embracing its burdensome regulations. The Spirit was directly challenging the Jews' prejudices, which served as obstacles to their full obedience of the Great Commission.

God used a vision to convince Peter that "God does not show favoritism but accepts from every nation the one who fears him and does what is right" (10:34–35; compare 10:9–16). By baptizing Cornelius and his household in the Holy Spirit, God wanted to convince the leaders in Jerusalem of the same thing. No one could argue with the clear logic that if God would give the Holy Spirit to Gentile believers, He must have accepted them as His people (10:47). Later when some Jewish Christians in Jerusalem criticized Peter for going to the Gentiles, he replied, "If God gave them the same gift he gave us who believed in the Lord Jesus Christ, who was I to think that I could stand in God's way?" (11:17). This argument convinced the Jewish Christians that God wanted them to proclaim the gospel to the Gentiles as well (11:18).

2. Gentiles can be empowered. A second reason Cornelius' household was baptized in the Holy Spirit was to empower them as Christ's witnesses in accordance with Jesus' promise in Acts 1:8. Explaining his actions to the Jewish leaders, Peter said: "As I began to speak, the Holy Spirit came on them as he had come on us at the beginning. Then I remembered what the Lord had said, 'John baptized with water, but you will be baptized with the Holy Spirit'" (Acts 11:15–17). Peter thus linked the Gentiles' experience to the missional promise of Jesus in Acts 1:4–8. These Gentiles received the same gift in the same way as the 120 on the Day of Pentecost did. Therefore, they must have received it for the same purpose—empowerment for witness.

3. Gentiles can join God's mission. A final reason God poured out His Spirit on Cornelius' household was to convince Jewish Christians that He has also called Gentiles to be full participants in His redemptive mission. It was not enough for Jewish Christians to accept Gentiles into the church; the Jews needed to know that Gentiles had been called to be witnesses for Christ just as they had. In the same way that salvation is for Jews and Gentiles alike, participation in God's mission is for both Jews and Gentiles.

Every time Christ baptizes someone in the Holy Spirit, He does so to empower that person as His witness. This story of the first Gentiles being empowered by the Holy Spirit highlights the truth that God wants every believer to participate in His all-important mission.

The Ephesian Disciples (Read Acts 19:1–7)

The fifth occurrence of Spirit baptism in Acts took place in the city of Ephesus. Paul visited the city during his third missionary journey. There, he found twelve disciples. These men likely came to faith through the preaching of Apollos and were members of the emerging church in Ephesus (Acts 18:24–28). Upon his arrival in Ephesus, Paul immediately asked them, "Did you receive the Holy Spirit when you believed?" (19:2).

Some people argue that Paul asked this question because he wanted to find out if these men were true believers. The argument goes like this: When a person is saved, they receive the Spirit (Romans 8:9). Therefore, when the twelve men answered, "No, we have not even heard that there is a Holy Spirit," Paul knew that they had not been born again. This prompted him to re-baptize them in water. Then, when Paul laid his hands on them, the Holy Spirit came on them and they were finally saved. This interpretation, however, ignores five facts:

1. The missional purpose of Spirit baptism. First, the argument ignores the missional purpose of the baptism in the Holy Spirit as defined by Jesus in Acts 1:4–8, a theme Luke consistently emphasized throughout Acts.

2. Luke's use of the word disciple. Next, the argument ignores the fact that these men were genuine Christian disciples when Paul met them. Luke used the word *disciple* twenty-nine other times in the book of Acts.[30] In every instance with one exception, the word clearly refers to Christian disciples. The one exception is Acts 9:25 where "his disciples" refers to disciples that Paul had made in Damascus. Nevertheless, this instance is still an indirect reference to Christian disciples since Paul's disciples were first and foremost disciples of Christ. It is therefore illogical to conclude that in this one isolated instance in 19:1, the author of Acts was referring to non-Christian disciples.

3. Paul's question. Third, the argument ignores the clear implication of Paul's question. The question "Did you receive the Holy Spirit when you believed?" implies that it is possible to believe and become a Christian without receiving the Holy Spirit, that is, in the Lukan sense of empowerment for mission. In Acts, "believed" is the key word describing how people become Christians.[31] Paul was clear in his teaching in Acts: "Believe in the Lord Jesus, and you will be saved" (Acts 16:31). Thus, Paul's question to the twelve Ephesian disciples makes sense only when Spirit baptism is understood as a distinct Christian experience with the purpose of empowerment for witness.

---

[30] See Acts 6:1, 2, 7; 9:1, 10, 19, 25, 26, 36, 38; 11:26, 29; 13:52; 14:20–22, 28; 15:10; 16:1; 18:23, 27; 19:1, 9, 30; 20:1, 30; 21:4, 16.

[31] Acts 4:4; 5:14; 8:12, 13; 9:42; 11:17, 21; 13:12, 48; 14:1; 17:12, 34; 18:7, 27; 19:2; 21:20.

4. The disciples' answer. Fourth, the argument ignores the response of the twelve disciples to Paul: "We have not even heard that there is a Holy Spirit" (Acts 19:2). Most likely, these words do not mean that these men had never heard of the existence of the Holy Spirit. Anyone who had any knowledge of the Old Testament would have heard of the Holy Spirit. Further, as disciples of John the Baptist, they would surely have heard that John proclaimed the Messiah would baptize His followers in the Holy Spirit (Matthew 3:11; Mark 1:8; Luke 3:16; John 1:33). Rather, the men's answer meant that they had not heard that the Holy Spirit had been poured out. Pentecostal scholar Stanley Horton notes that the Ephesian disciples' response to Paul's question could be translated literally: "But we have not even heard if the Holy Spirit is." He explains, "These disciples were really saying they had not heard about Pentecost or the availability of the baptism in the Holy Spirit."[32]

5. Paul's goal in Ephesus. Above all, to properly understand the Ephesian account, one must keep in mind that when Paul arrived in Ephesus, he came with a clear missionary goal in mind. His goal was not just to win a few converts to Christ—or even to plant a single church in Ephesus. Paul's goal was to plant churches throughout all of Asia Minor. This goal is revealed in Acts 19:10 where Luke wrote, "This went on for two years, so that all the Jews and Greeks who lived in the province of Asia heard the word of the Lord." Consequently, as Miller suggests, "Paul was not inquiring as to the twelve disciples' salvation. He was rather inquiring as to their readiness to participate in the mission of reaching Ephesus and Asia with the gospel."[33] In other words, Paul wanted to know if these men

---

[32] Stanley M. Horton, *Acts: A Logion Press Commentary*, rev. ed. (Springfield, MO: Gospel Publishing House, 2001), 318.

[33] Denzil R. Miller, *The Spirit of God in Mission: A Vocational Commentary on the Book of Acts* (Springfield, MO: PneumaLife Publications, 2011), 181.

had been empowered by the Holy Spirit because he wanted them to join him in reaching Asia Minor for Christ. If they were to join him, then they would need to be empowered by the Spirit just as he had been.

When Paul laid his hands on the Ephesian disciples, "the Holy Spirit came on them," just as Jesus had promised in Acts 1:8. As a result, "they spoke in tongues and prophesied" (19:6), just as the 120 and Peter had done on the Day of Pentecost. They were now ready to join Paul in his mission of reaching Asia for Christ.

Paul then took the disciples and immediately began to proclaim the kingdom of God in the local synagogue. Soon, he set up a school in the lecture hall of Tyrannus to train these and other workers to go to all parts of the province to proclaim the good news about Jesus and establish churches (Acts 19:9). Amazingly, after just two years, "all the Jews and Greeks who lived in the province of Asia heard the word of the Lord" (19:10). In this story, Luke once again highlighted the missional purpose of the baptism in the Holy Spirit.

Summary statement. From the above exercise, we conclude that the baptism in the Holy Spirit is a necessary biblical experience, distinct and separate from the new birth, whose primary purpose is empowerment for missional witness.

A Normative Experience

Scripture not only presents the baptism in the Holy Spirit as an empowering experience distinct from salvation, but it also presents it as a *normative* Christian experience. The term *normative* comes from the word *norm,* which means an authoritative, universal standard. Thus when we say that Spirit baptism is a normative experience, we are saying that not only *can* every believer be baptized in the Holy Spirit, but also that every believer *should* be baptized in the Holy Spirit. In other words, Spirit baptism is God's will for every believer. Three biblical concepts support this idea:

1. The promise of Joel. First, the promise of the Spirit that God gave through the prophet Joel was a universal promise: "In the last days, God says, I will pour out my Spirit on *all people*" (Acts 2:17, emphasis added; compare Joel 2:28). Peter further confirmed the normative nature of the promise when he declared, "The promise is…for all whom the Lord our God will call" (Acts 2:39).

2. The command of Jesus. Second, Jesus' final command to His church demonstrates that the experience is normative. Just before He returned to heaven, Jesus ordered His disciples: "Do not leave Jerusalem, but wait for the gift my Father promised, which you have heard me speak about. For John baptized with water, but in a few days you will be baptized with the Holy Spirit" (Acts 1:4–5). Jesus did not give His disciples a choice in the matter because He knew that without the Spirit's power, they would surely fail. The same is true today; without the Spirit's enablement, we will surely fail in our job of reaching others with the message of Christ. Therefore, the Bible commands us to "be filled with the Spirit" (Ephesians 5:18).

3. The purpose of the experience. Third, the experience of Spirit baptism is normative because of its missional purpose. This is perhaps the main reason God has commanded every one of His children to be baptized in the Holy Spirit. As this book has often emphasized, God is a missionary God, and He is on a mission to redeem and call to himself a people from every nation on earth. Furthermore, He has mandated that all of His children join Him in His mission. Left to our own devices, however, we would surely fail. We are weak and incapable of doing our part. The only way we can ever hope to succeed is with God's help. He gives us His help by empowering us with the Holy Spirit.

The book of Acts demonstrates how the early church understood the normative nature of Spirit baptism. Consequently, they insisted that every believer be empowered by the Holy Spirit (for example, 8:15–16; 9:17; 19:2–6). The church must continue to emphasize this apostolic mandate until the mission is completed and Christ returns.

ITS MISSIONAL NATURE

The baptism in the Holy Spirit is in essence a missionary experience. It is a powerful, life-changing encounter with God's missionary Spirit. The Bible uses at least six important terms to describe the experience. Each one highlights a different aspect of Spirit baptism and helps us understand the nature of the experience. When examined together, these terms and expressions provide a fuller understanding of the missional nature of the baptism in the Holy Spirit.

Baptism in the Holy Spirit

The phrase most often used to describe the experience is *baptism in the Holy Spirit*. When someone is properly baptized in water, the minister plunges that person into the water until he or she is completely immersed. In the same way, when Jesus baptizes individuals in the Holy Spirit, He plunges them into the Spirit until they are completely immersed in the presence and power of the Spirit. They are enveloped in, and overwhelmed by, God's missionary Spirit.

The New Testament uses the word *baptism* to describe a variety of experiences. The three most prominent of these are baptism in water, baptism into the body of Christ, and baptism in the Holy Spirit. Arrington observes, "In the performance of any baptism, there must be an *agent* who does the baptizing, the *element* in which the baptism occurs, and the *candidate* who is baptized."[34]

In the baptism in the Holy Spirit, Jesus is the agent who baptizes, disciples are the candidates who are baptized, and the Holy Spirit is the element in which they are immersed. John the Baptist made this clear when he declared, "I baptize you *with [in]* water, but he will baptize you *with [in]* the Holy Spirit" (Mark 1:8, emphasis added;

---

[34] French L. Arrington, *Christian Doctrine: A Pentecostal Perspective*, vol. 3 (Cleveland, TN: Pathway Press, 1994), 52.

compare Matthew 3:11; Luke 3:16; John 1:33). Jesus made the same point when He promised, "John baptized *with [in]* water, but in a few days you will be baptized *with [in]* the Holy Spirit (Acts 1:5, emphasis added; compare 11:16).

Some have mistakenly referred to the experience as "the baptism *of* the Holy Spirit." However, Scripture never uses that terminology. Using the preposition *of* incorrectly translates the Greek word *en* and infers that the Holy Spirit is the agent doing the baptizing, while on the contrary John the Baptist clearly identified Jesus as the baptizer in the Holy Spirit (John 1:33). In the New Testament, depending on the grammatical context, the Greek preposition *en* is usually translated as either "in" or "with" and sometimes as "by." In six of the seven New Testament verses where the verb *baptize* is connected with the Spirit, it is best translated as "in" or "with" (see Matthew 3:11; Mark 1:8; Luke 3:16; John 1:33; Acts 1:5; 11:16). The prepositions *in* and *with* correctly point to Jesus as the agent and the Holy Spirit as the element into which a person is baptized.

The seventh verse in the New Testament that connects the words *baptism* and *Spirit* requires special attention. Paul wrote, "For *by* one Spirit we were all baptized into one body, whether Jews or Greeks, whether slaves or free" (1 Corinthians 12:13, emphasis added, NASB). Here, rather than speaking about the baptism in the Holy Spirit as an empowering experience for God's mission, Paul was talking about baptism into the body of Christ, which happens at conversion. This verse identifies the Spirit as the agent who baptizes the believer into the body of Christ.

In Chapter 8 of this book, we discussed how the Spirit regenerates the repentant sinner and transforms that person into a new creation in Christ. At that moment, he or she is united with Christ and becomes a true child of God. This is the work of the Spirit that Paul was referring to in 1 Corinthians 12:13. The six other verses speak of a different experience that empowers believers for missional witness.

Being Filled with the Spirit

When a person is baptized in the Holy Spirit, in addition to being *immersed* in the Spirit they are also *filled with* the Spirit. The phrase *filled with the Spirit* is used seven times in the New Testament (Acts 2:4; 4:8, 31; 5:3; 9:17; 13:9, 52; Ephesians 5:18). Before Pentecost, Jesus commanded His disciples to stay in Jerusalem until they were "baptized with [in] the Holy Spirit" (Acts 1:5). When this happened, "All of them were *filled with the Holy Spirit* and began to speak in other tongues as the Spirit enabled them" (2:4, emphasis added). Miller explains how a single experience can be both a baptism and an infilling: "Just as an open container can, at the same time, be both immersed in and filled with water, so it was for these believers on the Day of Pentecost."[35] Thus, "baptized in the Spirit" and "filled with the Spirit" speak of different aspects of one empowering experience.

In Acts, the phrase "filled with the Spirit" is used to describe both the initial experience of Spirit baptism and subsequent empowerment experiences. At times, Christ's servants need a fresh supply of the Spirit's power to enable them for witness. Peter was first filled with the Spirit on the Day of Pentecost. A few days later, he was arrested and brought before the Jewish Sanhedrin. On that occasion, he was again "filled with the Spirit" and began to testify about Jesus (4:7–8).

Then once again, in an impromptu prayer meeting during a time of persecution, Peter and many others "were all filled with the Holy Spirit and spoke the word of God boldly" (Acts 4:31). This huge assembly included many who had already been baptized in the Holy Spirit on the Day of Pentecost and afterward (4:23). It also included others who on that occasion were filled with the Spirit for the first

---

[35] Denzil R. Miller, *Power Encounter: Ministering in the Power and Anointing of the Holy Spirit*, Revised. (Springfield, MO: AIA Publications, 2009), 60.

time. Luke used the same phrase to describe the experiences of both groups of people. All were enabled to testify boldly about Jesus.

The book of Acts further describes certain believers as being "full of the Spirit." For example, it describes both Stephen and Barnabas as being full of the Holy Spirit (6:5; 11:24). The phrase *full of the Holy Spirit* emphasizes a continuing state rather than a momentary experience.

Paul urged believers in Ephesus to "be [continually] filled with the Spirit" (Ephesians 5:18). This command suggests that it is possible for a person to be a Christian and not be full of the Spirit. This insight, along with the repeated fillings mentioned in Acts, shows that being filled with the Spirit is not a once-and-forever event. Just because a person was once "filled with the Spirit" does not necessarily mean that they are presently "full of the Spirit." To remain full of the Spirit, a person must actively seek, and regularly experience, spiritual renewal. We would do well to heed the following exhortation: "Pentecostals must not, and indeed cannot, rely on a past experience of having been filled with the Spirit. The decisive question is not 'When were you filled with the Spirit?' but rather 'Are you now filled with, and full of, the Spirit?'."[36]

The Spirit Coming On

In Acts 1:8, Jesus told His disciples that the Holy Spirit would "come on" them to empower them as His witnesses to the ends of the earth. Throughout his Gospel and Acts, Luke employs this "coming on" metaphor to describe the enabling work of the Holy Spirit.[37] While from time to time his terminology may vary slightly, it describes the same work of the Spirit. For instance, Luke speaks of

---

[36] Palma, *The Holy Spirit*, 179.

[37] Luke 1:35; 2:25; 3:21-22; 4:18; 24:49; Acts 1:8; 2:3, 17–18; 8:16–17; 10:44–45; 11:15; 19:6.

the Spirit's "clothing" individuals (Luke 24:49) or "resting" on them (Acts 2:3). Some translations might use "falling on" instead of "coming on." Whatever the wording, the picture is the same. The Holy Spirit comes on individuals to empower them and enable them to perform their God-given ministries.

You will remember that in Chapter 4, we discussed how the writers of the Old Testament often spoke of the Spirit coming on select individuals to empower them for ministry. In his writings, Luke used this same terminology to describe how the Spirit continues to come on people to empower them for Christian service. The idea of the Spirit's coming or falling on individuals emphasizes the missional purpose of the baptism in the Holy Spirit. The Spirit of Missions comes on us not to regenerate us and make us into Christians but to empower us and enable us for witness.

The Spirit Being Poured Out

The Scriptures also describe the baptism in the Holy Spirit as God's Spirit being "poured out" on one or more of God's children (Isaiah 32:15; 44:3; Ezekiel 39:29; Joel 2:28; Acts 2:17). This image corresponds well with the idea of the Spirit coming or falling on an individual, as discussed above. God "pours out" His Spirit. The Spirit then "comes on" and empowers the waiting disciple. The image of the Spirit being poured out also fits well with the idea of water being a symbol of the Holy Spirit. One Pentecostal scholar notes that the metaphor of the Spirit being poured out "suggests immersion such as would occur if one walked under a waterfall."[38] In other words, when a person is baptized in the Holy Spirit, he or she is flooded by the Spirit's power and presence.

The idea of God pouring out the Spirit further points to His promise to give His Spirit liberally to all His people. On the Day of

---

[38] Holdcroft, *The Holy Spirit: A Pentecostal Interpretation*, 92.

Pentecost, Peter explained what was happening by citing the prophecy of Joel: "This is what was spoken by the prophet Joel: 'In the last days, God says, I will pour out my Spirit on all people'" (Acts 2:16–17; compare Joel 2:28–32). This prophecy clearly connects the outpouring of the Spirit to God's mission. The Spirit is poured out on all God's people to enable them to "prophesy" (Acts 2:17–18), that is, to empower them to effectively proclaim the good news about Christ's salvation to the ends of the earth (Acts 1:8).

The Gift of the Holy Spirit

Scripture also refers to the baptism in the Holy Spirit as a *gift* from God (Acts 2:38; 8:20; 10:45; 11:17; 2 Timothy 1:6–7). More precisely, the Spirit is himself the gift. When someone is baptized in the Spirit, they receive more than an experience; they receive the very Person of the Spirit in a new and powerful way. Scripture calls the Holy Spirit a gift because God gives the Spirit to us freely. Jesus promised, "Your Father in heaven [will] give the Holy Spirit to those who ask him!" (Luke 11:13). No one can earn or purchase this gift. Only God can give the gift of the Holy Spirit, and He offers it freely to all His children. They must simply ask in faith. In the next chapter, we will take a deeper look at how a person may receive this wonderful gift.

The Promise of the Father

A final expression used in Scripture to describe the baptism in the Holy Spirit is *the promise of the Father* (Luke 24:49; Acts 1:4; 2:33). In the Bible, God has promised His children many wonderful blessings. However, when the Bible talks about *"the* promise of the Father," it refers to the gift of the Holy Spirit, which God first showered on His church on the Day of Pentecost.

God had previously announced the promise in the Old Testament through such prophets as Isaiah, Ezekiel, and Joel (Isaiah 32:15; 44:3;

Ezekiel 39:29; Joel 2:28). Jesus repeated the promise several times during His ministry. Once He told His disciples, "I am going to send you what my Father has promised" (Luke 24:49). He then commanded them to "wait for the gift my Father promised, which you have heard me speak about" (Acts 1:4; compare Luke 24:49; John 7:37–39; 14:16–17, 26; 16:7).

This promise of the Holy Spirit is a universal promise. It is no longer for a select few, as it was in the Old Testament. Peter quoted Joel to explain the outpouring of the Spirit at Pentecost:

> In the last days, God says,
> I will pour out my Spirit on *all people.*
> Your *sons* and *daughters* will prophesy,
> your *young men* will see visions,
> your *old men* will dream dreams.
> Even on my *servants*, both *men* and *women,*
> I will pour out my Spirit in those days,
> and they will prophesy.
> (Acts 2:17–18, emphasis added; compare Joel 2:28–29)

The promise is for everyone: sons and daughters, young and old, men and women, rich and poor. God's wants to empower all His people so that they may join Him in His mission of reaching the nations.

Because the gift of the Spirit is a *promise* from God, any follower of Jesus can confidently ask for it, knowing that their heavenly Father delights in giving the gift to His children. On the Day of Pentecost, Peter announced to the attentive crowd, "The promise [of the Holy Spirit] is for you and your children and for all who are far off—for all whom the Lord our God will call" (Acts 2:39).

IMPLICATIONS AND APPLICATIONS

Jesus insisted that His followers be empowered by the Holy Spirit. They receive this empowering when they are baptized in and filled with the Spirit. The book of Acts presents this powerful spiritual experience as being distinct and separate from salvation. It is the next essential Christian experience following salvation. The primary purpose of Spirit baptism is to empower God's people to witness. Because Jesus requires every believer to participate in His mission, He requires each one to be baptized in the Holy Spirit. The apostles understood these truths, and they diligently taught them to others.

We must also teach believers today about the inseparable connection between advancing God's mission and the empowerment of the Holy Spirit. Jesus emphasized this connection in His final message before returning to heaven. He said to His disciples, "You will receive power when the Holy Spirit comes on you; and you will be my witnesses in Jerusalem, and in all Judea and Samaria, and to the ends of the earth" (Acts 1:8). Luke continued to emphasize the connection throughout the book of Acts. Until the mission is completed, every follower of Christ is commanded to be baptized in the Holy Spirit.

Emphasizing Spirit baptism is essential to mobilizing the church for effective evangelism, church planting, and missions. When God's people are baptized in the Holy Spirit, they receive the power they need to carry the gospel message to others. Pastors and church leaders must therefore teach and preach often on the subject, and they must give their people many opportunities to receive the gift. Such a strategy will stimulate people's faith to receive the Holy Spirit. It will further help move them into action as Christ's witnesses. I pray that you will grasp the importance of this experience, and that you will commit yourself to receiving the Spirit and leading other believers into the same experience.

In this chapter, we have examined the nature and missional purpose of the baptism in the Holy Spirit. In the next chapter, we will continue our examination of the subject by looking at the missional signs that accompany Spirit baptism. We will also discuss how a person can receive this powerful spiritual experience.

Questions for Discussion and Reflection

1. How should Jesus' command that his followers be baptized in the Holy Spirit affect our preaching and teaching in the church?

2. How would you respond to the idea that the baptism in the Holy Spirit is not a separate empowering experience but simply another term for being born again?

3. How would you respond to the idea that the baptism in the Holy Spirit with the evidence of speaking in other tongues is an experience God will give to some believers but not all believers?

4. How might emphasizing the baptism in the Holy Spirit serve as an essential element in mobilizing God's people for evangelism, church planting and missions?

~ CHAPTER 10 ~

Baptism in the Holy Spirit: Its Missional Signs

In the previous chapter, we learned that the baptism in the Holy Spirit is an experience of divine power given by God to enable His people to effectively participate in His redemptive mission. We also learned how the missional purpose of Spirit baptism makes it an essential experience for every follower of Christ. In this chapter, we will examine some additional truths concerning Spirit baptism. First, we will explore the missional signs that accompany the experience. Second, we will discuss how every believer can receive the baptism in the Holy Spirit. In doing this, we will discover that the Spirit is best received in a context of commitment to God's mission.

When a follower of Christ is baptized in the Holy Spirit, certain observable evidences will invariably accompany and authenticate the experience. We refer to these evidences as *missional signs* because each one is directly connected to the missional purpose of Spirit baptism.

In the book of Acts, each time believers were baptized in the Holy Spirit, their experience was verified by two identifiable missional signs. First, through the Spirit's enablement, they spoke in other tongues. Then through the same enablement, they began to witness for Christ with great power, just as Jesus had promised in Acts 1:8. Both signs are foundational to the biblical experience of Spirit baptism.

The examples of Spirit baptism presented in Acts are important because, in writing Acts, Luke was presenting his readers with more than a mere history of the early church. He wrote to give them the model of how the church must advance to the ends of the earth in the power of the Holy Spirit to accomplish God's mission before the return of Christ. God's people are empowered by being baptized in the Holy Spirit. Luke was also careful to show the essential elements involved in receiving the Spirit and then ministering in the Spirit's power.

SPEAKING IN TONGUES AS A MISSIONAL SIGN OF SPIRIT BAPTISM

The book of Acts demonstrates that when disciples are baptized in the Holy Spirit, they speak in tongues as the Spirit enables. In Acts, Luke presented five examples of people being initially filled with the Spirit evidenced by speaking in tongues. Three of the accounts contain an explicit reference to speaking in tongues (2:1–4; 10:44–47; 19:1–6). The other two strongly imply that the recipients spoke in tongues (8:14–17; 9:17–18). We will consider each of these incidents.

Three Explicit Examples

1. The Day of Pentecost (Acts 2:1–4). The disciples' experience at Pentecost serves as a paradigm—or lasting model—of Spirit baptism. The "sound like the blowing of a violent wind" and the "tongues of fire" were unique occurrences that were never repeated again. However, what came after the wind and the fire established a pattern that is repeated throughout the book. Luke stated, "All of them were filled with the Holy Spirit and began to *speak in other tongues,* as the

Spirit enabled them" (Acts 2:4, emphasis added). This pattern of people being filled with the Spirit and then immediately speaking in tongues and being empowered for witness is echoed throughout Acts.

2. Cornelius' Household (Acts 10:44–46). Another outpouring of the Spirit occurred at Cornelius' house in the city of Caesarea. In his description of this event, Luke again explicitly states that those who received the Spirit spoke in tongues: "The circumcised believers who had come with Peter were astonished that the gift of the Holy Spirit had been poured out even on Gentiles. *For they heard them speaking in tongues* and praising God" (Acts 10:45–46, emphasis added). The fact that the recipients spoke in tongues convinced Peter and his Jewish companions that these Gentiles had received the gift of the Holy Spirit just as the 120 had on the Day of Pentecost (11:15). In this account, speaking in tongues was the indisputable proof that the Gentile believers had been baptized in the Holy Spirit.

3. The Twelve Disciples in Ephesus (Acts 19:1–7). The third account of speaking in tongues in Acts took place in the city of Ephesus, about twenty-five years after the Day of Pentecost. When Paul arrived in Ephesus, he met twelve disciples. After talking with them, he laid his hand on them, and "the Holy Spirit came on them, and *they spoke in tongues* and prophesied" (Acts 19:6, emphasis added). Just as had happened in Jerusalem and Caesarea, these Ephesian believers spoke in tongues as evidence of being baptized in the Holy Spirit.

Two Implicit Examples

In addition to the three examples in Acts where the text explicitly states that those who were filled with the Holy Spirit spoke in tongues, two additional examples strongly imply the same.

4. The Samaritan Converts (Acts 8:14–17). There is no explicit mention of the new believers in Samaria speaking in tongues when they received the Holy Spirit. There is, however, an indication that a dramatic sign accompanied their being filled. Luke wrote, "When Simon saw that the Spirit was given at the laying on of the apostles' hands, he offered them money and said, 'Give me also this ability so that everyone on whom I lay my hands may receive the Holy Spirit'" (8:18–19). Simon saw something that impressed him so much that he offered money to the apostles to give him the power to do what he had seen them do. Most New Testament scholars, both Pentecostal and non-Pentecostal, acknowledge that Simon most likely saw the Samaritan believers speaking in tongues, just as other recipients of the Spirit had done throughout the book of Acts.

5. Saul of Tarsus (Acts 9:17–18). On the road to Damascus, Saul encountered the risen Christ. Three days later, God sent a disciple named Ananias to pray for him. When Ananias laid hands on Saul, the apostle-to-be was "filled with the Holy Spirit" (Acts 9:17–18). While the text does not explicitly state that he spoke in tongues, from Paul's own letters we know that he regularly spoke in tongues (1 Corinthians 14:18). It is therefore reasonable to conclude that Paul began speaking in tongues when he was initially filled with the Spirit, as did others in the book of Acts. Just as the twelve Ephesian disciples spoke in tongues when Paul laid hands on them, it is likely that Paul spoke in tongues when Ananias laid hands on him.

Initial Physical Evidence

These five examples from the book of Acts show how Scripture closely connects speaking in tongues with Spirit baptism. Pentecostal scholars have noted this connection and have traditionally referred to speaking in tongues as the "initial physical evidence" that a person has been baptized in (and filled with) the Holy Spirit.

The word *initial* points to the fact that speaking in tongues is the first confirming evidence that a person has been baptized in the Holy Spirit. It also implies that tongues are not the only evidence. A further confirming evidence that a person has been baptized in the Holy

Spirit is Spirit-empowered missional witness, as we will discuss later in this chapter. The word *physical* points to the fact that speaking in tongues is an outward visible evidence of an inner spiritual transformation that has occurred in the life of the recipient.

The Nature of Speaking in Tongues

A careful examination of the experience of the 120 disciples on the Day of Pentecost helps us understand what happens when a newly Spirit-filled believer speaks in tongues. From the account of Acts 2, we learn three important truths about the nature of speaking in tongues:

1. A Supernatural Experience. First, we learn that speaking in tongues is a supernatural experience. It is possible only through the divine enablement of the Holy Spirit. At Pentecost, the 120 were filled with the Holy Spirit and began to speak in other tongues "as the Spirit enabled them" (Acts 2:4). Empowered by the Spirit of God, these early believers began to speak supernaturally in languages previously unknown to them. The same thing happens when a Spirit-filled believer speaks in tongues today.

2. A Real Language. Second, we learn that speaking in tongues is an authentic language. Those filled with the Spirit on the Day of Pentecost spoke in actual living languages (Acts 2:7–11). When a Spirit-filled believer speaks in tongues, he or she is speaking in a real language. Scripture reveals that it might be a human language or a heavenly language (1 Corinthians 13:1).

3. A Cooperative Effort. Third, from the Pentecost story, we learn that speaking in tongues is a cooperative effort between the Spirit of God and the Spirit-filled disciple. When the Spirit came on the disciples at Pentecost, they sensed His powerful presence filling them. Then, responding to the inner prompting of the Spirit, they "began to speak in other tongues as the Spirit enabled them" (Acts 2:4). Notice that the disciples participated with the Holy Spirit in what happened.

The Spirit did not force them to speak against their will. He prompted and enabled them, and they spoke out in obedient faith as the Holy Spirit supernaturally enabled them to speak the words He gave them. They were not speaking from their own minds and thoughts. Rather, they were speaking the words the Holy Spirit inspired them to say in a language unknown to them. Even though they did not understand what they were saying, they submitted themselves to the Holy Spirit and continued to speak in faith. In the same way, any believer today who wishes to be baptized in the Holy Spirit must also be ready and willing to act in faith and cooperate with the Holy Spirit.

Luke's Teaching on the Missional Nature of Tongues

Three New Testament authors mentioned speaking in tongues in their writings: Luke, Paul, and Mark. Each one makes an important contribution to our understanding of how speaking in tongues relates to the *missio Dei*. From the writings of Luke, we learn three things about the missional nature of speaking in tongues.

A Fulfillment of Prophecy

First, Luke made it clear that tongues are a missional fulfillment of Old Testament prophecy. On the Day of Pentecost, 120 disciples were baptized in the Holy Spirit and began to speak in other tongues as the Spirit enabled them (Acts 2:1–4). Peter then stood and explained that this outpouring of the Spirit resulting in Spirit-inspired speech was a fulfillment of an ancient prophecy. He declared, "This is what was spoken by the prophet Joel: 'In the last days, God says, I will pour out my Spirit on all people'" (Acts 2:16–17; compare Joel 2:28–29). In other words, in the last days God would pour out His Spirit on people of all nations and ethnicities, renewing them and empowering them to participate in His mission.

Chapter 10 ~ Baptism in the Holy Spirit: Its Missional Signs

Prophetic Speech

Next, Luke showed the missional nature of tongues by identifying it as prophetic speech. When the crowd heard the disciples speaking in tongues, they were amazed, and asked, "What does this mean?" (Acts 2:12). Peter answered them by quoting from the prophecy of Joel, who wrote, "In the last days, God says, I will pour out my Spirit on all people. Your sons and daughters *will prophesy*...Even on my servants, both men and women, I will pour out my Spirit in those days, and *they will prophesy*" (Acts 2:17-18, emphasis added). Luke thus identified speaking in tongues as a form of prophetic speech.[39] The final verse of the prophecy quoted by Peter identifies the purpose of the prophetic speech as missional by declaring "and everyone who calls on the name of the Lord will be saved (2:21).

In the Old Testament, a prophet was someone whom God anointed with the Holy Spirit to deliver His message to people. By connecting speaking in tongues with prophecy, Luke was declaring that all who are baptized in the Holy Spirit as evidenced by speaking in tongues have been commissioned and empowered by God to prophetically proclaim the message of salvation to the nations.

A Normative Missional Sign

In Acts, Luke showed that those who were empowered by the Holy Spirit spoke in tongues. However, Luke presented tongues as more than a mere evidence that one has been baptized in the Holy Spirit. He presented tongues as a "normative missional sign" pointing to God's mission to redeem the nations through Spirit-empowered proclamation of the gospel.

---

[39] Roger Stronstad explains that by quoting Joel, Peter "identifies the disciples experience of 'speaking in other tongues as the Spirit gave utterance' (Acts 2:4) to be prophetic speech. *The Prophethood of All Believers: A Study in Luke's Charismatic Theology* (New York: Sheffield Academic Press, 2003), 69.

Luke illustrated the missional symbolism of tongues by purposefully linking speaking in tongues to God's mission. In discussing the events of Pentecost, Miller points out:

> After describing the disciples' Spirit-enabled speaking in tongues in Acts 2:4, Luke immediately informs his readers, "Now there were dwelling in Jerusalem Jews, devout men *from every nation under heaven*" (v. 5, emphasis added)." He then lists 15 Gentile languages spoken by those who had just received the Spirit (vv. 6–11).[40]

By doing this, Luke confirmed that speaking in tongues was a missional sign indicating that the disciples had been empowered by the Spirit to take the gospel to the nations. Today, when a person is filled with the Spirit and speaks in tongues, we should be reminded of God's mission to redeem the nations and that He has given us His Spirit to empower us to participate effectively in that mission.

Paul's Teaching on the Missional Nature of Tongues

In 1 Corinthians 12–14, Paul presents two distinct uses of tongues. First, he discusses the role of tongues as a prayer language for all believers. Then, he talks about tongues as a spiritual gift that operates in the local church. As we examine Paul's teaching about tongues, it is important to keep this distinction in mind. It is also important to realize that both kinds of tongues have strong missional implications.

---

[40] Denzil R. Miller, *Missionary Tongues Revisited: More Than an Evidence: Recapturing Luke's Missional Perspective on Speaking in Tongues* (Springfield, MO: PneumaLife Publications, 2014), 58.

A Personal Prayer Language

Prayer in tongues is a powerful method of communicating with God. Paul wrote that, when a person prays in tongues, he or she speaks to God (1 Corinthians 14:2). Using himself as an example, Paul identified two ways a person can pray: with the mind and with the Spirit. He wrote, "If I pray in a tongue, my spirit prays, but my mind is unfruitful. So what shall I do? I will pray with my spirit, but I will also pray with my understanding" (vv. 14-15).

When Spirit-filled believers pray in tongues, they are not praying their own thoughts as they would in normal prayer. They are praying under the inspiration, and by the enablement, of the Holy Spirit (1 Corinthians 14:14). Paul mentioned this kind of prayer when he urged the Ephesian believers to "pray in the Spirit on all occasions" (Ephesians 6:18). Because we are weak, we need the Spirit's help to pray. Paul explained:

> The Spirit helps us in our weakness. We do not know what we ought to pray for, but the Spirit himself intercedes for us through wordless groans. And he who searches our hearts knows the mind of the Spirit, because the Spirit intercedes for God's people in accordance with the will of God. (Romans 8:26–27)

A Congregational Gift

In addition to being a prayer language, speaking in tongues can function as a congregational gift. It is one of several manifestations of the Spirit given as gifts to the local church (1 Corinthians 12:8–11). At times, God will use tongues to communicate a prophetic word to the church (12:10; 14:26). For such a message in tongues to benefit the church, it must be interpreted. Then, everyone can understand what is being said and can be edified (14:6–13, 26–28). A message in tongues followed by an interpretation functions as a word of prophecy to the church (14:5).

Either the person who gave the message in tongues or another Spirit-filled believer can give the interpretation (1 Corinthians 14:13, 27). Paul further taught that, if there is no one to interpret, while a person can continue to pray in tongues, he or she should do so softly in a manner that does not disrupt the worship service (14:28).

Paul gave these guidelines because some believers in the Corinthian church were abusing the gift of tongues. These individuals evidently viewed speaking in tongues as a superior gift. They were speaking in tongues in a way that caused confusion and created disorder in the worship services (1 Corinthians 14:33). Speaking in tongues with interpretation is meant to be a blessing to the church. However, when the gift is misused, it can create problems. A wise pastor will never allow this to happen.

Paul's intention in giving these instructions was not to suppress speaking in tongues nor to hinder the moving of the Spirit in any way. Rather, it was to motivate God's people to allow the Spirit to work through them to edify the church in an orderly manner. That is why Paul concluded with this exhortation, "Therefore, my brothers and sisters, be eager to prophesy, and do not forbid speaking in tongues. But everything should be done in a fitting and orderly way" (1 Corinthians 14:39–40).

Every local church needs the ministry of the Holy Spirit. Therefore, pastors and church leaders should teach and encourage their people concerning the proper use of the spiritual gifts, including the gifts of tongues and interpretation. In their fear of the misuse of *some* gifts, some pastors have closed the door to the manifestation of *any* gift in their churches. We must never make this grave mistake.

Tongues are Universally Available

Paul further affirmed that tongues are available for every believer. His goal was that every believer might speak in tongues often. He testified, "I thank God that I speak in tongues more than all of you"

(1 Corinthians 14:18). In addition, he encouraged the Corinthians, "I would like every one of you to speak in tongues" (v. 5).

Some non-Pentecostal theologians use Paul's instructions to argue that the apostle taught that tongues are not for all believers. They note how Paul asked the Corinthians, "Are all apostles? Are all prophets? Are all teachers? Do all work miracles? Do all have gifts of healing? *Do all speak in tongues?* Do all interpret?" (1 Corinthians 12:29–30, emphasis added). They point out that the obvious answer to Paul's question is, "No, everyone does not speak in tongues." In this way, they conclude that Paul taught that speaking in tongues is not for every believer.

When Paul asked these questions, however, he was dealing with the proper use of spiritual gifts in the church when believers gathered for worship (1 Corinthians 14:23, 26). He was not referring to the use of tongues as a prayer language or as a sign of Spirit baptism. While it is true that not everyone will give a message in tongues or its interpretation in a worship service, it is also true that God can use any Spirit-filled believer to manifest any gift He chooses (12:11).

As we have already discussed, Luke demonstrates in the book of Acts that the baptism in the Holy Spirit, confirmed by speaking in tongues, is a promise for every believer. This is because every believer needs to be empowered by the Spirit to speak for Christ as a witness to the lost. Therefore, Paul wanted every believer to speak in tongues (1 Corinthians 14:5).

Tongues are Valuable

Unlike many misguided teachers today, Paul taught that speaking in tongues has great value, and that believers should desire to speak in tongues. This is because when someone prays in tongues, that person is strengthened inwardly. Paul said, "Anyone who speaks in a tongue edifies themselves" (1 Corinthians 14:4). When believers pray in tongues, they are spiritually renewed and strengthened by the Spirit's power and presence. At the same time, they are empowered by the Spirit to be effective witnesses for Christ (Acts 1:8). Furthermore, they are built up in their faith and kept in the love of God (Jude 20–21).

Tongues are a Sign to Unbelievers

Finally, Paul taught that tongues can serve as a sign to unbelievers (1 Corinthians 14:22). In this way, tongues have a clear missional purpose, even when they occur in a gathering of God's people. In such contexts, tongues can serve as a sign to unbelievers in at least two ways.

First, when a message in tongues is given and followed by an interpretation, the prophetic word can bring conviction to the heart of unbelievers. This produces the same effect as a word of prophecy. Unbelievers are "convicted of sin…and the secrets of their hearts are laid bare. So they will fall down and worship God, exclaiming, 'God is really among you!'" (1 Corinthians 14:24–25).

A second powerful way that tongues may serve as a sign to unbelievers is when a Spirit-filled believer speaks in a language he or she does not know, yet unbelievers hear the person speaking in their own native language. This is what happened on the Day of Pentecost. The 120 "unlearned Galileans" miraculously spoke in the languages of the surrounding Gentile nations—and their hearers understood them (Acts 2:7–11). Occasionally this happens today. In his book *Spoken by the Spirit,* Ralph W. Harris has documented testimonies of this spiritual phenomenon occurring around the world.[41] When this does happen, it becomes a powerful testimony to unbelievers of the reality of God's power and presence. It opens their hearts to God and often draws them to repentance and faith in Christ.

---

[41] Ralph W. Harris, *Spoken by the Spirit: Documented Accounts of "Other Tongues" from Arabic to Zulu* (Springfield, MO: Gospel Publishing House, 1973).

Chapter 10 ~ Baptism in the Holy Spirit: Its Missional Signs

Mark's Teaching on the Missional Nature of Tongues

Along with Luke and Paul, Mark is another biblical author who addressed the issue of speaking in tongues. In the final lines of his Gospel, Mark quoted the words of Jesus as He issued His Great Commission:

> Go into all the world and preach the gospel to all creation. Whoever believes and is baptized will be saved, but whoever does not believe will be condemned. And these signs will accompany those who believe: In my name they will drive out demons; *they will speak in new tongues;* they will pick up snakes with their hands; and when they drink deadly poison, it will not hurt them at all; they will place their hands on sick people, and they will get well. (Mark 16:15–18, emphasis added)

Mark tells us two important things about speaking in tongues:

Believers Should Expect to Speak in Tongues

Jesus declared, "These signs will accompany those who believe: In my name…they will speak in new tongues" (Mark 16:17). Speaking in tongues is a divinely appointed sign of believers in Christ. Those who put their faith in Him should expect to be filled with the Spirit and used in supernatural ways, including speaking in tongues.

Tongues are Missional

In His Great Commission, Christ connected tongues to His mandate to declare the gospel "in all the world" (16:15). Speaking in tongues thus plays an important role in the fulfillment of Jesus' command to evangelize the nations in the Spirit's power. As disciples go to the nations to preach the good news, they should expect that the Holy Spirit will empower them to speak boldly and to work miracles in Christ's name (Acts 1:8; 2:4, 43). They should further expect that all who believe in Christ will be empowered by the Spirit with the "normative missional sign" of speaking in tongues. These new Spirit-empowered disciples will then join in the work of evangelizing the nations.

SPIRIT-EMPOWERED WITNESS AS A MISSIONAL SIGN OF SPIRIT BAPTISM

The book of Acts portrays Spirit-empowered witness as another missional sign that always accompanies a person's being baptized in the Holy Spirit. Based on His promise in Acts 1:8, the primary reason Jesus baptizes disciples in the Holy Spirit is to empower them for effective witness. Spirit baptism accompanied by Spirit-inspired speaking in tongues should always lead to Spirit-empowered proclamation of the gospel. A recurring pattern in Acts demonstrates this to be true. Without exception, every time the Holy Spirit came on and filled believers, they began to witness in the Spirit's power. In other words, empowered proclamation of the gospel followed speaking in tongues in each of the five accounts of Spirit baptism in Acts.

Pentecost

A careful reading of the Pentecost story reveals that on that day, Peter spoke by the Spirit two times. First, he spoke in tongues along with the rest of the 120 believers (Acts 2:4). Then, he spoke by the Spirit a second time when he powerfully proclaimed the gospel to the crowd that had gathered (2:14–40). As a result, 3,000 people came to faith in Christ (2:41). At Pentecost, a lasting pattern for Spirit baptism was established—Spirit-inspired speaking in tongues followed by Spirit-empowered proclamation of the gospel.

Chapter 10 ~ Baptism in the Holy Spirit: Its Missional Signs

Samaria

When the believers in Samaria were baptized in the Holy Spirit, they spoke in tongues (implied in Acts 8:15–19). They also began to witness, resulting in more people in Samaria and in neighboring regions being won to the Lord. Luke wrote, "Then the church throughout Judea, Galilee and Samaria enjoyed a time of peace and was strengthened. Living in the fear of the Lord and encouraged by the Holy Spirit, it increased in numbers" (Acts 9:31).

Paul

In Damascus, Paul was filled with Holy Spirit and spoke in tongues (Acts 9:17–18, implied). Then "at once he began to preach in the synagogues that Jesus is the Son of God" (9:20). And he "grew more and more powerful and baffled the Jews living in Damascus by proving that Jesus is the Messiah" (9:22).

The Household of Cornelius

In Caesarea, the Gentile converts also spoke by the Spirit in two ways, they were heard "speaking in tongues and praising God" (Acts 10:46). The Christian Standard Bible translates this verse, "For they heard them speaking in other tongues and *declaring the greatness of God*" (emphasis added). In other words, those who received the Spirit in Caesarea not only spoke in tongues under the inspiration of the Spirit, they proclaimed the greatness of God in the common language.

The Ephesian Disciples

When Paul laid hands on the twelve Ephesian disciples, "they spoke in tongues and prophesied" (Acts 19:6). Again, two kinds of Spirit-inspired speaking are emphasized—tongues and prophecy. In the book of Acts, prophecy includes Spirit-empowered proclamation of the gospel. In Ephesus, this Spirit-inspired witness did not happen just this one time, for Paul along with the twelve Ephesian disciples "entered the synagogue and spoke boldly there for three months, arguing persuasively about the kingdom of God" (19:8). The apostle also established a training school in a local lecture hall where he taught and mobilized the ever-growing number of disciples. "This went on for two years, so that all the Jews and Greeks who lived in the province of Asia heard the word of the Lord" (19:10).

The apostolic pattern demonstrated in the book of Acts shows that when people are genuinely filled with the Spirit, they speak in tongues followed by Spirit-empowered proclamation of the gospel. Therefore, we should preach and teach that a truly biblical experience of Spirit baptism will result in both Spirit-inspired speaking in tongues and Spirit-empowered proclamation of the gospel.

Additionally, we should teach that just as a believer must cooperate with the Spirit to speak in tongues, he or she must cooperate with the Spirit to witness in His power. The same Holy Spirit who fills us and enables us to speak in tongues will fill us and enable us to witness with power. However, we must do our part. In both instances, we must speak by faith as the Holy Spirit enables us.

RECEIVING THE HOLY SPIRIT

Thus far in this lesson, we have learned many important truths about the baptism in the Holy Spirit. For these truths to affect our lives, however, we must each personally experience the baptism in the Holy Spirit. This is God's promised gift to all His children; yet He instructs us to ask Him for the gift.

We will now consider how we may receive and be filled with the Holy Spirit.

Who Can Receive the Gift of the Holy Spirit

Who can receive the promised gift of the Holy Spirit? Scripture speaks of one basic prerequisite, a person must be a child of God (John 14:17). Jesus told His disciples, "If you then, though you are evil, know how to give good gifts to your children, how much more will your Father in heaven give the Holy Spirit to those who ask him!" (Luke 11:13).

On the Day of Pentecost, Peter emphasized this truth by declaring, "Repent and be baptized, every one of you, in the name of Jesus Christ for the forgiveness of your sins. And you will receive the gift of the Holy Spirit" (Acts 2:38). He is saying that anyone who has become a child of God by repenting of their sins and putting their faith inChrist, is a candidate to be baptized in the Holy Spirit. This is an important point to emphasize when teaching on the baptism in the Holy Spirit. No one who loves and serves Jesus should have any doubt in their heart that God will give them this wonderful gift. They need only ask Him for it (Luke 11:13).

How to Receive the Gift of the Holy Spirit

Jesus spoke of four factors that prepare believers to receive the gift of the Holy Spirit: desire, consecration, faith, and prayer. Believers can therefore prepare themselves to receive the Holy Spirit by cultivating these qualities in their lives.

Desire

Jesus used the images of hunger and thirst to teach about the role of desire in receiving the Holy Spirit. In the Sermon on the Mount, He said, "Blessed are those who hunger and thirst for righteousness, for they will be filled" (Matthew 5:6). On another occasion, Jesus promised the Spirit to those who deeply desire for Him to work in their lives:

> Jesus stood and said in a loud voice, "Let *anyone who is thirsty* come to me and drink. Whoever believes in me, as Scripture has said, rivers of living water will flow from within them." By this he meant the Spirit, whom those who believed in him were later to receive. (John 7:37–39, emphasis added)

Consecration

Consecration to Christ and His mission is a second important element for being baptized in the Holy Spirit. Jesus declared: "If you love Me, you will keep My commandments. I will ask the Father, and He will give you another Helper, that He may be with you forever; that is the Spirit of truth..." (John 14:15–17, NASB). God does not offer His Spirit to enable us to fulfill our own selfish desires. He gives His Spirit to empower us to fulfill His mission. Above all else, the candidate for Spirit baptism must be committed to Christ and His mission to redeem the nations.

The apostles took this responsibility very seriously. When they were threatened and ordered to stop testifying in Jesus' name, they responded, "We must obey God rather than human beings...We are witnesses of these things, and so is the Holy Spirit, *whom God has given to those who obey him"* (Acts 5:29, 32, emphasis added). They knew that God gives the Holy Spirit to those who obey Christ and are committed to declaring the gospel message. The proper context for receiving the Holy Spirit is in the context of commitment to Christ and to His mission.

Faith

Faith is a third requisite for receiving the gift of the Holy Spirit. Jesus emphasized that we receive the Holy Spirit by believing in Him. Speaking of the Holy Spirit, He said, "Whoever believes in me, as Scripture has said, rivers of living water will flow from within them" (John 7:38). Paul stated succinctly, "By faith we...receive the promise of the Spirit" (Galatians 3:14).

Faith is the key that opens the door to receive the gift of the Spirit from God. Jesus taught, "Whatever you ask for in prayer, believe that you have received it, and it will be yours" (Mark 11:24). Therefore, when we ask God to give us the Holy Spirit, we must do so with faith, believing that He has heard and answered our prayers.

Prayer

Committed prayer is the fourth essential element for receiving the Holy Spirit. Jesus taught His disciples to ask for this gift:

> So I say to you: Ask and it will be given to you; seek and you will find; knock and the door will be opened to you. For everyone who asks receives; the one who seeks finds; and to the one who knocks, the door will be opened.... If you then, though you are evil, know how to give good gifts to your children, how much more will your Father in heaven give the Holy Spirit to those who ask him! (Luke 11:9–10, 13)

A person does not receive the gift of the Holy Spirit automatically or casually. Any believer who desires to be filled with the Spirit must determine to pray. They must sincerely ask Jesus to baptize them in the Holy Spirit.

In the original Greek text, the commands to ask, seek, and knock are present-tense commands, which indicates the need for continual prayer. So we must *keep* asking, *keep* seeking, and *keep* knocking. This means that we must be serious and persist in prayer. At the same time, Jesus added a wonderful promise to His command to pray. He said "everyone who asks receives" (11:10). When we ask God for the gift of the Holy Spirit, we can do so with confidence, knowing that God hears and answers our prayers.

REMAINING FULL OF THE HOLY SPIRIT

Being baptized in the Holy Spirit marks the believer's entry into a Spirit-filled life. However, once a believer has been baptized in the Holy Spirit, they must endeavor to remain full of the Spirit. For what is the value of being filled with the Spirit if a believer does not remain full of the Spirit?

The book of Acts describes believers as being both "filled with" (2:4; 4:8, 31; 9:17) and "full of" (6:3, 5; 7:55; 11:24) the Holy Spirit.

Filled with speaks of the empowering experience; *full of* speaks of the resulting state. Acts further shows that the early disciples had repeated fillings with the Spirit. For example, Peter was first filled with the Spirit at Pentecost (Acts 2:4). He was filled again in 4:8, and again in 4:31. We, too, should seek and anticipate repeated fillings with the Spirit.

Paul exhorted the Galatian believers to continue in their Spirit-filled walk. "Since we live by the Spirit," he said, "let us keep in step with the Spirit" (Galatians 5:25). He further urged the Ephesian believers to "be [continually] filled with the Spirit" (Ephesians 5:18). In the Greek New Testament, Paul's command to "be filled" is in the present tense. This means that being filled with the Spirit is both an initial event and an ongoing experience. Thus, we must continually allow the Holy Spirit to fill us. We can do this by living in a state of constant openness to Him and by following the instructions that Jesus gave to His disciples to "keep asking" for the Holy Spirit (Luke 11:9).

The Spirit of God is the Christian's source of power for life and ministry. This explains why Paul urged Timothy, his son in the faith, to be renewed by the Holy Spirit. He wrote, "For this reason I remind you to fan into flame the gift of God, which is in you through the laying on of my hands. For the Spirit God gave us does not make us timid, but gives us power, love and self-discipline" (2 Timothy 1:6–7). Paul then encouraged Timothy, "Do not be ashamed of the testimony about our Lord.... Rather, join with me in suffering for the gospel, by the power of God" (1:8). Paul knew that if Timothy was to share his faith effectively with others, he would need to continually fan into flame the Spirit's presence in his life. It is the same for us today. A fire being used for cooking needs constant attention. In the same way, we must constantly tend to the flame of the Spirit in our hearts.

How can we fan into flame the presence and power of the Spirit in our lives, and thereby ensure that we remain full of the Holy Spirit?

To do this, we must continue to cultivate the four elements we examined earlier in our discussion: desire, consecration, faith, and prayer. These four elements, which are central to being baptized in the Holy Spirit, are also essential to remaining full of the Spirit. How do each of these four practices helps us remain full of the Holy Spirit?

Desire

A believer who has been filled with the Holy Spirit must constantly remain desirous of the Spirit's empowering. When Jesus said that those who hunger and thirst for righteousness will be filled, He was talking about continued hungering and thirsting (Matthew 5:6). In other words, those who continually hunger and thirst after God will experience the Spirit's continued infilling.

Consecration

God's Spirit will abide in those who remain consecrated to God and committed to His mission. This consecration will manifest itself in holy living and selfless concern for others. God identified Jesus to John as "the man on whom you see the Spirit come down and remain" (John 1:33). One reason the Spirit remained on Jesus was that He always remained committed to His Father's will. Jesus testified, "I seek not to please myself but him who sent me" (5:30). If we too want to remain full of the Spirit, we must follow Jesus' example by remaining committed to the Father and His mission.

Faith

We receive the Spirit by faith, as we learned earlier. We also live the Spirit-empowered life by faith. Both the filling of the Spirit and the Spirit-empowered ministry that results are products of faith in Christ. Paul asked the Galatian Christians, "Does God give you his Spirit and work miracles among you by the works of the law, or by your believing what you heard?" (Galatians 3:5). The answer is that God's Spirit works miraculously through those who believe.

Prayer

Speaking of the gift of the Holy Spirit, Jesus exhorted His disciples, "Ask [or keep on asking] and it will be given to you" (Luke 11:9). The promises of Jesus in the next verse that "everyone who asks receives" and "the one who seeks finds" are also in the present tense. This indicates that the one who keeps on asking also keeps on receiving. The one who keeps on seeking also keeps on finding (11:10). Clearly, the Spirit-filled life is daily nourished and sustained by prayer.

If we will continue to long for the Spirit in our lives and stay committed to Christ and His command to witness, our hearts will remain open to God. We will then be ready at all times for God to fill us continually with the Spirit. All along, we must live by faith and persist in prayer asking God to fill us with His Spirit (Luke 11:9–13). If we will do this, God will continually fill us with His Spirit.

IMPLICATIONS AND APPLICATIONS

In this chapter, we have learned that the Bible presents the baptism in the Holy Spirit as a powerful last-days missional experience. Jesus promised, "You will receive power when the Holy Spirit comes on you; and you will be my witnesses…to the ends of the earth" (Acts 1:8). Like the experience itself, its accompanying sign of speaking in tongues also has powerful missional implications. It is vital that every follower of Christ understand these implications.

Speaking in tongues is the "initial physical evidence" that one has been baptized in the Holy Spirit. However, it is more than that. In Acts, tongues are also presented as the *normative missional sign* that a person has been empowered by the Holy Spirit to speak for Christ. Luke, Paul, and Mark each demonstrated the missional nature of speaking tongues.

Because of its missional purpose, being baptized in the Holy Spirit is an essential experience for every follower of Christ.

Chapter 10 ~ Baptism in the Holy Spirit: Its Missional Signs

Unfortunately, many Pentecostal leaders and pastors no longer emphasize the experience. They often downplay the practice of speaking in tongues. Consequently, most people who attend Pentecostal churches today have not been baptized in the Holy Spirit according to the biblical pattern of Acts 2:4. We must once again emphasize the importance of the baptism in the Holy Spirit and its accompanying sign of Spirit-enabled speaking in tongues.

However, we must go beyond emphasizing speaking in tongues as the sign of Spirit baptism. In addition, we must emphasize the even more important result of Spirit-empowered witness. Believers who spoke in tongues but did not witness for Christ were unheard of in the New Testament church. It should be the same in the church today.

Questions for Discussion and Reflection

1. In light of the book of Acts, is speaking in tongues a necessary part of being baptized in the Holy Spirit and why?

2. How might a lack of emphasis on speaking in tongues affect the church's effectiveness in evangelism and missions?

3. In light of the book of Acts, how should we respond when believers speak in tongues but do not engage in witnessing to the lost?

4. Based on the principles in this lesson, how would you respond to a person who prayed and asked God to fill them with the Holy Spirit but was not filled with the Spirit with the evidence of speaking in tongues?

5. Based on the principles in this lesson, how would you respond to a person who was filled with the Spirit and spoke in tongues in the past but no longer prays in other tongues?

Chapter 10 ~ Baptism in the Holy Spirit: Its Missional Signs

~ CHAPTER 11 ~

MINISTRY IN THE SPIRIT

Throughout our study, we have emphasized how the Holy Spirit is a missionary Spirit. His work on earth is centered on fulfilling the *missio Dei*. We have further stressed that the empowerment of the Spirit is essential for God's people to effectively fulfill their role as witnesses both at home and around the world. Through His exemplary ministry, Jesus demonstrated that our witness must be done in the power of the Holy Spirit. Authentic New Testament ministry must contain an element of the supernatural (Matthew 4:23; 9:35; 10:1, 8; Luke 10:9; John 14:12).

In addition to Spirit-empowered witness to the lost, every believer is called to participate in the ministry of spiritual gifts in the church when believers are gathered for worship (Romans 12:5–8; Ephesians 4:12–16). In this final chapter, we will examine the role of spiritual gifts in ministry and missions. We will conclude with practical instructions concerning the vital ministry of praying with believers to be filled with the Holy Spirit.

SPIRITUAL GIFTS

Ministry in the Spirit takes place when the Holy Spirit ministers through believers in the operation of spiritual gifts. Paul wrote to the church in Corinth, "When you come together, each of you has a hymn, or a word of instruction, a revelation, a tongue, or an interpretation. Everything must be done so that the church may be built up" (1 Corinthians 14:26). The manifestation of spiritual gifts characterized ministry in the New Testament church. It should be the pattern in the church today as well.

God desires for every believer to be empowered by His missionary Spirit. He also desires for them to be used in the manifestation of spiritual gifts (1 Corinthians 12:7). While each believer may have areas of natural gifting, spiritual gifts go beyond such natural abilities. They are Holy Spirit-enabled capabilities. Spiritual gifts can be defined as "supernatural anointings given by the Spirit of God through Spirit-filled believers to accomplish the will of the Father."[42] Spiritual gifts are manifested when the Spirit of God comes on believers, filling them and enabling them to perform beyond their natural capabilities. Further, spiritual gifts are given to accomplish God's will. Above all else, God's will includes fulfilling His mission of saving the lost and building His church among all nations. As we have noted throughout this study, this mission can only be accomplished through the Spirit's enablement. Spiritual gifts are essential to the supernatural ministry to which every follower of Christ has been called.

In 1 Corinthians 12:7–10, Paul lists nine gifts (or manifestations) of the Spirit:

---

[42] Denzil R. Miller, *In Step with the Spirit* (Springfield, MO: AIA Publications, 2008), 185.

> Now to each one the manifestation of the Spirit is given for the common good. To one there is given through the Spirit the message of wisdom, to another the message of knowledge by means of the same Spirit, to another faith by the same Spirit, to another gifts of healing by that one Spirit, to another miraculous powers, to another prophecy, to another distinguishing between spirits, to another speaking in different kinds of tongues, and to still another the interpretation of tongues.

Later in the same letter, Paul wrote, "Where there are prophecies, they will cease; where there are tongues, they will be stilled; where there is knowledge, it will pass away. For we know in part and we prophesy in part, but when completeness comes, what is in part disappears" (1 Corinthians 13:8–10). Some non-Pentecostal theologians have wrongly interpreted this passage to mean that these supernatural gifts of the Spirit ceased with the completion of the New Testament canon and the death of the last apostle. However, the arrival of completion that Paul spoke of in this passage will only take place at the end of the age when Christ returns to establish His eternal kingdom. Earlier in the epistle, Paul told the Corinthian believers, "You do not lack any spiritual gift as you eagerly wait for our Lord Jesus Christ to be revealed" (1:7). The Spirit gives gifts to enable disciples to minister in His strength until Jesus returns from heaven. Christ has commissioned His church to be His witnesses to "the ends of the earth" (Acts 1:8). As long as this commission remains in effect, the enablement of the Spirit, with all of His gifts and enablements, will also remain in effect.

Identifying Spiritual Gifts

In addition to the list above, the New Testament contains four other lists of spiritual gifts. All five lists are presented in Table 11.1. Take a few moments to read the five passages mentioned and familiarize yourself with the spiritual gifts presented in each. Keep in mind that each gift is manifested as the Holy Spirit works in and through Spirit-filled believers, enabling them in ministry. (Note: Many Bible Scholars feel that the grammatical structure of Ephesians 4:11 indicates that the leadership gifts of pastor and teacher are a combined gift, pastor-teacher, rather than two separate gifts.)

Table 11.1

Five Lists of Spiritual Gifts in the New Testament	

Romans 12:6–8
    Prophesying
    Serving
    Teaching
    Encouraging
    Giving
    Leading
    Showing Mercy
	1 Corinthians 12:28–31
	    Apostles
	    Prophets
	    Teachers
	    Workers of miracles
	    Gifts of healing
	    Helping
	    Guidance/Administration
	    Different kinds of tongues
	    Interpretation of tongues

1 Corinthians 12:8–10
    Message of wisdom
    Message of knowledge
    Faith
    Gifts of healing
    Miraculous powers
    Prophecy
    Distinguishing between spirits
    Different kinds of tongues
    Interpretation of tongues
	Ephesians 4:11
	    Apostles
	    Prophets
	    Evangelists
	    Pastors and Teachers
	
	1 Peter 4:10–11
	    Speaking
	    Serving

General Observations

We can make six general observations about spiritual gifts. These observations will help orient us as we examine the gifts in more detail.

The Lists Are Not Comprehensive

When we say the gift lists are not comprehensive, we mean that they do not contain every gift the Spirit may choose to give to believers. This is supported by the fact that none of Paul's four lists are identical. Horton observes, "The emphasis is on the fact that all come from the one Holy Spirit, not that all the gifts are being named."[43] We can, however, be certain of one thing. All the gifts listed are important and necessary for the church to fulfill its reason for being.

Some of the Named Gifts Are a Ministry Role

Some gifts do not identify actions but rather individuals whom the Spirit enables to fulfill a more permanent ministry, role, or function. These gifts could include apostles, prophets, evangelists, pastors, and teachers. They refer to individuals God has called and the Spirit has anointed for specific ministry roles. The Spirit may use these individuals to manifest a variety of spiritual gifts as they carry out their ministry roles. In this chapter, however, we will focus our comments primarily on the gifts presented as Spirit-anointed actions. We do this because those are the gifts that the Holy Spirit may choose to manifest through any Spirit-filled believer at any time. He does this to carry out God's will for the church and to advance His mission in the earth.

---

[43] Horton, *What the Bible Says About the Holy Spirit*, 209.

Some of the Named Gifts May Reflect Broad Categories

Rather than being interpreted narrowly as a single gift, some of the gifts named may be interpreted more broadly as a group or class of gifts. These groups might include a wide range of functions. For instance, leading, serving, helping, speaking, and showing mercy seem to be this type of broad gift. At the same time, other gifts may be more specific, such as prophesying, discerning of spirits, speaking in tongues, and teaching.

It Is Helpful to Place Gifts into Groups

While the New Testament writers do not group the spiritual gifts, most New Testament scholars find that placing related gifts into logical groupings can be useful. Since the five lists of gifts are likely representative rather than comprehensive, organizing them into such categories helps us understand their meaning and function. Such an exercise can offer insight into various ways in which the Spirit works through Spirit-filled believers to accomplish the will of God. Table 11.2 on the next page presents a suggestion of how the gifts might be grouped.

The Gifts Are Named but Not Defined

In the five gift lists mentioned in Romans, 1 Corinthians (two times), Ephesians, and 1 Peter, spiritual gifts are named, but nowhere in these or any other New Testament epistle are they clearly defined. In 1 Corinthians 12–14, Paul presents his most comprehensive instructions concerning spiritual gifts and their operation in the church. Yet even there, he offers no clear definition or demonstration of any gift. This insight compels us to move with humility as we define each of the spiritual gifts and discuss how they operate in the church.

Table 11.2

Possible Groupings of Spiritual Gifts
Gifts of Power (Spirit-energized works) • Faith • Gifts of healing • Miraculous powers *Gifts of Revelation* (Spirit-conferred insight) • Message of wisdom • Message of knowledge • Distinguishing between spirits *Gifts of Proclamation* (Spirit-inspired speech) • Prophecy • Different kinds of tongues • Interpretation of tongues • Teaching • Encouraging *Gifts of Stewardship and Service* (Spirit-enabled service) • Serving • Giving • Administration • Showing mercy *Gifts of Leadership* (Spirit-called and -empowered leadership) • Apostles • Prophets • Evangelists • Pastor-teachers

Chapter 11 ~ Ministry in the Spirit

We must not, however, allow this fact to discourage us from eagerly seeking to be used in the exercise of spiritual gifts. After all, Paul does exhort believers to "eagerly desire gifts of the Spirit" (1 Corinthians 14:1). We should be encouraged that there are many examples of the gifts in operation in the Gospels and Acts. These examples are found in the Spirit-anointed ministry of Jesus (Luke 4:18–19; Acts 10:38) and in the Spirit-empowered ministries of the apostles and other disciples in the book of Acts (Acts 4:33). A careful examination of these books in light of the five categories of gifts suggested in Table 11.2 reveals many such examples. Table 11.3 lists a few of the many incidences of spiritual gifts in operation in Acts, and it would be valuable to study each of these examples.

Table 11.3

Examples of Spiritual Gifts in Operation in Acts	
Spiritual Gift	**Examples in Acts**
• Prophecy:	
ο Proclamation	4:8–12; 31, 33
ο Foretelling	11:28; 21:4, 10–11
• Message of knowledge	5:3–4; 8:23
• Message of wisdom	6:10; 15:13–21
• Tongues	2:4; 10:46; 19:6
• Faith	3:4–7, 16; 6:5; 11:24
• Gifts of healing	3:6–7; 8:7; 28:8–9
• Miraculous powers	9:36–41; 20:9–10
• Distinguishing between spirits	16:16–18
• Giving	2:45; 4:34–37
• Showing mercy	9:36
• Administration/Leadership	6:1–7

We Should Value Every Spiritual Gift

A final observation we may make is that we should highly value spiritual gifts. This is because each gift has a significant role to play in the body of Christ. As mentioned earlier, Paul urged the Corinthian Christians to "eagerly desire the greater gifts" (1 Corinthians 12:31). In saying this, Paul did not mean that some gifts are more important than others, or that some gifts are to be cherished while others are to be cast aside. On the contrary, he was saying that we should not emphasize one gift to the exclusion of other gifts that the church may need at any given time.

Throughout his teaching in 1 Corinthians, Paul emphasized a wide variety of spiritual gifts. He further stressed that all the gifts are necessary to build up the church (12:4–7; 14:12, 26). He urged the Corinthian believers, "Since you are eager for gifts of the Spirit, try to excel in those that build up the church" (14:12). What is most needed to build up the church will vary from situation to situation. Therefore, whichever gift best enables the church to fulfill God's will in a situation is at that moment the "greatest gift." The Spirit stands ready to supply every need and enable the church to accomplish God's will effectively. Our priority, therefore, should be to remain full of the Holy Spirit and humbly submit ourselves to His leading in the exercise of the gifts.

Purposes of Spiritual Gifts

Spiritual gifts are essential in every aspect of church life and ministry. They are needed when the church gathers for worship and when the church moves out in mission. In other words, gifts are needed to build up the body of Christ by ministering to the believers when they come together to worship God. They are also vital to the work of advancing God's kingdom on the earth by enabling disciples to witness with power and to plant Christ's Spirit-empowered church among the nations. Paul emphasizes the first purpose in his epistles, and Luke emphasizes the second purpose in Acts.

Strengthening the Church

A primary purpose for spiritual gifts is to supernaturally enable believers to strengthen and encourage one other, and thus build up the body of Christ. Paul emphasizes this important purpose on three separate occasions where he wrote about spiritual gifts (Romans 12:4–8; 1 Corinthians 12:1–14:33; Ephesians 4:11–16). He explains, "To each one the manifestation of the Spirit is given for the common good" (1 Corinthians 12:7). The gifts are not given for the personal benefit or exaltation of the person through whom they are manifested. Rather, they are given that we may bless and serve one another. Peter explains, "Each of you should use whatever gift you have received to serve others, as faithful stewards of God's grace in its various forms...so that in all things God may be praised through Jesus Christ" (1 Peter 4:10–11).

Every follower of Christ must be equipped for Spirit-filled ministry in the local church. It is therefore essential that we teach believers about the nature, purpose, and proper operation of spiritual gifts. We must also show them how the Holy Spirit can use them in the manifestation of these gifts. The Pentecostal pastor and other church leaders are responsible for developing believers in these areas. Paul noted that Christ gives spiritual leaders to the church "to equip his people for works of service" (Ephesians 4:12).

The pastor can begin by desiring to see spiritual gifts in operation in the church and by accepting the responsibility to cultivate their use. The pastor can do this by teaching the church what the Bible says about spiritual gifts and how they are to function in the local assembly. The pastor can further encourage the use of spiritual gifts in the Body by modeling authentic Spirit-empowered ministry before the people.[44]

---

[44] For insights on how to encourage and guide believers in the proper and beneficial use of spiritual gifts within a local church, see chapter 8,

Advancing the Kingdom

The second purpose of spiritual gifts, which is often overlooked, is to advance the kingdom of God in evangelism, church planting, and missions. We miss this purpose when we focus solely on Paul's teaching on spiritual gifts in his epistles while ignoring Luke's teaching in his Gospel and Acts. Paul's teaching on spiritual gifts focuses almost entirely on the role of spiritual gifts in the church gathered for worship. However, as has already been demonstrated in this study, the book of Acts offers many examples of spiritual gifts in operation in the church scattered in mission. The majority of these examples in Acts are connected to the advancement of the gospel among the spiritually lost.

In Acts, Luke used some form of the term "signs and wonders" eleven times (2:19, 22, 43; 4:30; 5:12; 6:8; 7:36; 8:6, 13; 14:3; 15:12). This phrase indicates the miraculous operation of spiritual gifts in the context of gospel proclamation. In one of his summary statements in Acts, Luke noted how "everyone was filled with awe at the many wonders and signs performed by the apostles" (Acts 2:43). The most prominent of these signs was the manifestation of the gift of healing. Such manifestations were central to the advancement of the gospel. They often opened the door for effective proclamation of the gospel.

Not only did the Spirit use the apostles to perform miracles, healings, and exorcisms, He also used other believers to do the same. For instance, He used the Spirit-filled "deacons" Steven and Philip in performing healings and miracles among the people (Acts 6:8; 8:6–7). In addition, the Spirit used a "disciple" named Ananias to bring healing to the recently converted Saul of Tarsus and to lead him into the experience of Spirit baptism (9:10–18). Ananias' Spirit-anointed action was instrumental in preparing Saul to begin his powerful ministry for Christ (9:17–22).

"Pastoring the Spiritual Gifts," in the Discovery Series book, *Power Ministry: How to Minister in the Spirit's Power,* by Denzil R. Miller.

The proclamation gifts also played a prominent role in the advancement of the gospel in Acts. These prophetic utterances include speaking in tongues, Spirit-empowered proclamation of the gospel, and other prophetic words. For example, on the Day of Pentecost, the 120 spoke in tongues "as the Spirit enabled them" (2:4). Peter then stood, and under the same inspiration, boldly proclaimed the gospel to the multitude that had gathered. As a result, the people were "cut to the heart" (2:37), and 3,000 "accepted his message" and were saved (2:41).

The book of Acts also contains examples of spiritual gifts being manifested in the context of the church gathered in worship (for example, 6:1–4; 11:28; 13:1–4; 20:9–11). For instance, the gifts of leadership and administration are evidenced in the story of the choosing of seven deacons in Acts 6:1–6. This Spirit-guided action served to resolve a conflict that had engulfed the church and distracted them from their primary task of witness. The manifestation of these gifts enabled the church to regain focus on the mission and resulted in continued growth and evangelistic success (6:7). Whether the gifts of the Spirit were manifested in the church or in the marketplace, the ultimate result was increased effectiveness in evangelism, church planting, and missions.

Furthermore, the manifestation of the gift of prophecy was often instrumental in mobilizing the church and guiding believers into missionary outreach. This truth was especially evident in the church in Antioch. As a result of a prophetic message in the assembly, Paul and Barnabas were launched into their first missionary journey (Acts 13:2–3). It is also likely that through prophetic messages, Paul and his missionary band were guided by the Spirit into Europe (16:6–7), which ultimately led them to plant the first churches in the European continent. These are just a few of the many examples in Acts of how spiritual gifts were essential in advancing God's kingdom.

Exercising Spiritual Gifts

The Spirit of God can use any Spirit-filled disciple in the ministry of spiritual gifts. Paul wrote concerning spiritual gifts that "to each one the manifestation of the Spirit is given for the common good" (1 Corinthians 12:7). These gifts are not given to the individual believer as a possession. Neither are they given for personal blessing. Rather, gifts are the manifestation of the Spirit's powerful working through Spirit-filled believers for the benefit of others. The Spirit can therefore use any Spirit-filled believer at any time to manifest any gift in order to fulfill any purpose He chooses. Our responsibility is simply to remain full of the Spirit and to be ready to respond to His promptings. Our need is to receive the Spirit and then allow Him to manifest His gifts through us as He chooses.

The Scriptures identify at least six elements necessary to prepare Spirit-filled believers to be used in the ministry of spiritual gifts:

1. Understanding

To be effectively used in the ministry of spiritual gifts, a believer must first understand the nature, purpose, and function of the gifts. Paul exhorted the Corinthian believers, "Now about gifts of the Spirit, brothers and sisters, I do not want you to be uninformed" (1 Corinthians 12:1). The Corinthians were not "uninformed" in the sense that they did not know *about* the spiritual gifts, for Paul had already said to them, "You do not lack any spiritual gift" (1:7). Instead, they were uninformed about the purpose and proper operation of the gifts. The believers in Corinth were manifesting spiritual gifts, but unfortunately, their improper use of the gifts was harming rather than helping the church. Paul wrote to teach them how the gifts were to function properly in the church.

As previously mentioned, Luke also wrote about spiritual gifts; however, he taught using a narrative style. While Paul discussed the proper operation of the gifts in the church gathered in worship, Luke presented the proper operation of the gifts in the church scattered in mission.

What was true in the Corinthian church in Paul's time is true for the church today. Many Christians are ignorant about spiritual gifts. Before we can see the gifts in operation in our churches—and in our own lives and ministries—it is crucial that we address this ignorance. We must teach God's people about spiritual gifts. We must help them know about the existence and availability of these gifts. We must further teach them how they can respond to the Spirit in order to be used in the manifestation of spiritual gifts both in the church and in the harvest field.

2. Desire

If believers are to be used in the manifestation of spiritual gifts, they must, in the words of Paul, "eagerly desire gifts of the Spirit" (1 Corinthians 14:1). In addition, believers must "try to excel in [gifts] that build up the church" (14:12). The Spirit of God will not force himself on anyone. He comes and moves where He is wanted. Therefore, for the Spirit to use us in the ministry of spiritual gifts, we must open our hearts to the Spirit and invite Him to use us. We do this because we love the church and we want to see it strengthened. We also love the lost and want to see them won to Christ.

3. Humility

Spiritual gifts can only be properly used in a spirit of true humility. In Paul's discussion of spiritual gifts in Romans, he warned, "Do not think of yourself more highly than you ought, but rather think of yourself with sober judgment, in accordance with the faith God has distributed to each of you" (12:3). If God uses us to manifest spiritual gifts, we must frequently remind ourselves that we are merely "jars of clay" through whom the Spirit works (2 Corinthians 4:7). We must also remember that we are Christ's servants whom He has called to deny ourselves, take up our cross, and follow Him (Luke 9:23).

4. Submission

To be used in the ministry of spiritual gifts, a believer must submit to the Spirit. Paul wrote that spiritual gifts "are the work of one and the same Spirit, and he distributes them to each one, *just as he determines*" (1 Corinthians 12:11, emphasis added). We must keep in mind that the gifts belong to the Holy Spirit and not to us. The Spirit therefore manifests himself through us *according to His will*, not ours. This demands that we submit ourselves to Him. When we are engaged in ministry—whether worship, evangelism, or missions—different contexts demand different gifts. One gift is appropriate to one context, while another gift is appropriate to another context. The Spirit knows best which gift is needed to meet the need of the moment. We must submit ourselves to the Spirit and seek to be led by Him so that He can manifest through us the gift He chooses.

5. Obedience

If believers are to be used in the manifestation of spiritual gifts, they must also understand the vital role of obedience. As we walk in the Spirit, there will be times when the Spirit will prompt us to do or say something. At such times, He may be urging us to exercise a certain spiritual gift. If we ignore the Spirit's prompting, nothing happens. However, if we choose to obey, He comes to anoint us for ministry.

This principle is illustrated in Jesus' Great Commission in Mark 16. There, Jesus spoke of the manifestation of spiritual gifts. He promised, "These signs will accompany those who believe: In my name...they will place their hands on sick people, and they will get well" (Mark 16:17–18). In this context, the manifestation of the gift of healing is connected to obedience to Jesus' command to "go into all the world and preach the gospel to all creation" (16:15). Jesus was saying that as we obey Him and go preach the gospel, He will send the Spirit to anoint us and work miracles through us. The Spirit of

God anoints us as we act in obedience to the Word of God and to the Spirit's inner promptings.

6. Faith

The anointing that comes as we obey the Spirit and the Word is released by an act of faith. Jesus said, "These signs will accompany those who believe" (Mark 16:17). Paul explained to the Romans that we manifest spiritual gifts "in accordance with the faith God has distributed to each of [us]" (Romans 12:3). He also said that a person prophesies in accordance with his or her faith (12:6). James added, "The prayer offered in faith will make the sick person well; the Lord will raise them up" (5:15). This is how it works: The Spirit prompts us to do or say something. As we obey, the Spirit anoints us for ministry. We must then act in faith, saying or doing what the Spirit has commanded. As we act in faith, the gift is manifested and the work is accomplished.

Being used in spiritual gifts is a partnership between the Spirit and the Spirit-empowered disciple. Paul wrote, "The spirits of prophets are subject to the control of prophets" (1 Corinthians 14:32). In other words, the prophet can cooperate with the Spirit and manifest the spiritual gift, or the prophet can resist the Spirit and suppress the gift. The Holy Spirit never takes control of believers in the sense of manipulating or forcing them to speak or act. Only evil spirits do that. We must choose to obey the Spirit's prompting and speak or act in faith. The Holy Spirit will then anoint us and enable us to minister in His power.

An example of this kind of faith is illustrated in the story of the healing of the lame man in Lystra. As Paul was preaching, the Holy Spirit revealed to him that this man believed the message and that he "had faith to be healed" (Acts 14:9). Paul then had to make a choice. He could ignore the Spirit, or he could respond in bold faith. Paul chose to act in faith and commanded the man, "Stand up on your feet!" Hearing Paul's words, "the man jumped up and began to walk"

(14:10). As Paul exercised his faith and obeyed the prompting of the Spirit, the gift of healing was released and the man was healed. Not only that, but the whole city received a powerful witness verifying the truth of Paul's message.

PRAYING WITH BELIEVERS TO RECEIVE THE HOLY SPIRIT

The early church made it a priority to pray with new Christians to be filled with the Holy Spirit. Jesus established this priority in His final command before returning to heaven. He ordered His disciples, "Do not leave Jerusalem, but wait for the gift my Father promised, which you have heard me speak about. For John baptized with water, but in a few days you will be baptized with the Holy Spirit" (Acts 1:4–5). Jesus knew that their success in mission would depend on the presence and power of the Spirit in their lives.

The apostles followed Jesus' example. When they heard that Samaria had received the gospel, they immediately sent Peter and John to the Samaritans to pray for them that "they might receive the Holy Spirit" (Acts 8:14–15). Later, when Saul of Tarsus was saved, God sent Ananias to pray with him that he might receive the Holy Spirit (9:17). And when Paul arrived in Ephesus, the first question he asked the disciples there was, "Did you receive the Holy Spirit when you believed?" (19:2). He then prayed with them to receive the Spirit.

As spiritual leaders, we too have been called to mobilize our churches for Spirit-empowered ministry, missions, and church planting. Before our church members can minister in power, they must be baptized in—and thus empowered by—the Holy Spirit (Acts 1:1–8). It is the responsibility of every minister of the gospel to lead others into the baptism in the Holy Spirit. In this final section of our study, we will address this important topic.

Getting Ready to Minister

Any Spirit-filled Christian can pray with another Christian to receive the Holy Spirit. The story of Ananias praying for Saul demonstrates this truth. Ananias had no official ministry position. The Bible simply calls him a "disciple" (Acts 9:10). And yet, God used him to lead a future apostle into the baptism in the Holy Spirit.

How can we do the same? How can we lead other brothers and sisters in Christ into the experience of Spirit baptism? There are a couple of things we must do before attempting to lead others into Spirit baptism:

1. Prepare ourselves. We begin by preparing ourselves to pray with others to receive the Spirit. It is good to memorize some key Scriptures concerning Spirit-baptism. We cited many such Scriptures in Chapter 10 where we discussed receiving the Holy Spirit. You can use these Scriptures to teach and encourage those seeking to be empowered by the Spirit. You should also allow the Lord to refill you with the Holy Spirit. As you pray with the candidate, you should remain prayerful and sensitive to the Spirit's leading.

2. Believe God's promise. God promised, "In the last days…I will pour out my Spirit on all people" (Acts 2:17). While teaching His disciples about the Holy Spirit, Jesus applied the promise: "Ask and it will be given to you; seek and you will find; knock and the door will be opened to you. For everyone who asks receives" (Luke 11:9–10). In concluding His Pentecost sermon, Peter announced, "The promise is for you and your children and for all who are far off—for all whom the Lord our God will call" (Acts 2:39).

Since it is God's job to give people the Spirit, as you pray with the seeker, do not worry about the results. Simply believe God's promise. Remember, the results do not depend on you. Your job is simply to lead the seeker in prayer and to trust God to fulfill His promise.

Instructions before Prayer

Before praying with seekers, take a few moments to offer some instructions and helpful information. As you instruct them, keep in mind the four important elements in receiving the Holy Spirit mentioned in Chapter 10, including desire, consecration, faith, and prayer. Share pertinent Scriptures and instructions to encourage the seekers and to build their faith to receive the Spirit.

In Africa, many people believe that their spiritual leaders possess special powers. They go to these leaders expecting to receive help and blessings from them. This idea may lead some to put their faith in their pastors and other ministers rather than in God. It may also cause them to wait passively for something to happen to them as they are being prayed for. That is why it is important to remind the seeker that the heavenly Father gives the Holy Spirit to those who diligently ask Him in faith (Luke 11:13 with Mark 11:24).

As you instruct seekers, it is helpful to explain to them the three "steps of faith" they can take in receiving the Holy Spirit:

1. *Ask in faith.* The first step is to ask for the Holy Spirit. Jesus promised, "Ask and it will be given to you" (Luke 11:9). Encourage seekers by saying, "When you ask, believe that God is keeping His promise, and that He is giving you the Holy Spirit. Remember, Jesus promised that the Holy Spirit will 'come on' us (Acts 1:8). When the Spirit comes, you will sense His presence."

2. *Receive in faith.* Once seekers begin to sense the Spirit's presence on them, they will need to take a second step of faith. In faith, they should invite the Holy Spirit to come inside them and fill them. Jesus said, "Everyone who asks *receives*" (Luke 11:10, emphasis added). He also instructed, "Whatever you ask for in prayer, *believe that you have received it*, and it will be yours" (Mark 11:24, emphasis

added). Encourage seekers to open their hearts fully to God and to receive the Holy Spirit by faith. Lead them in this prayer: "Jesus, fill me with the Holy Spirit. Right now, by faith, I receive the Holy Spirit!" The candidates should now believe that they *have received!*

3. *Speak in faith.* Once seekers truly believe, they will sense the Spirit's stirring inside of them. They will now need to take a final step of faith. They must begin to speak out in faith from where they sense the Spirit's presence within (John 7:38). As the 120 disciples did on the Day of Pentecost, they should begin to speak the words the Holy Spirit gives them. As they do, they will begin to "speak in other tongues as the Spirit enable[s] them" (Acts 2:4). This will be an act of faith. These seekers will need to trust the Holy Spirit and begin to speak, not their own words, but rather the words He gives them.

Prayer to Receive the Spirit

The time has now come to pray with the seekers to receive the Holy Spirit. In doing this, consider the following:

1. *Leading them in prayer.* Pray with the candidates, leading them in the three steps of faith described above. It is helpful to lead the seekers in each step, much as you would lead a sinner in the sinner's prayer. As you do this, encourage them to reach out to God in sincerity and faith. Once you have led them in prayer, urge them to continue praying. They should focus on sensing the Spirit's presence. Once they sense His presence inside them, they should begin to speak out in faith, trusting the Spirit to give them the words. During the entire procedure, remain patient yet lovingly persistent.

2. *Laying on of hands.* It is often helpful to lay hands on seekers as you pray for them. This was a common practice in the

book of Acts (8:17–18; 9:17; 19:6). God sometimes used Spirit-filled believers to lay hands on new believers as they prayed with them to receive the Holy Spirit. We should remember, however, that the gift of the Holy Spirit is "the gift of God" (Acts 8:20; 2 Timothy 1:6–7). Only He can give the Holy Spirit. We should also remember that laying on of hands is not a requirement for receiving the Spirit. No one laid hands on the believers on the Day of Pentecost (Acts 2:4), nor did Peter lay hands on those whom the Spirit fell upon in Caesarea (10:44).

3. *After-prayer instructions*. After praying, it is important to instruct and encourage those who have been seeking the Spirit. Remind those who have received that God gave them the Spirit to empower them as Christ's witnesses to the lost. Encourage them to begin witnessing for Jesus immediately, trusting the Holy Spirit to empower and direct them. You should further encourage them to endeavor to be filled with the Spirit daily. If some seekers you prayed with did not receive the Spirit as evidenced by speaking in tongues, encourage them to continue seeking to be filled. Let them know that the promise is true and that it is indeed for them (Acts 2:17–18, 38–39). Jesus said, "Everyone who asks receives" (Luke 11:10). If they will keep on asking, seeking, and knocking—and they will act in faith—they too will soon be filled with the Holy Spirit.

IMPLICATIONS AND APPLICATIONS

God's mission to save the lost and build the church can only be accomplished in God's power using God's methods. Authentic New Testament ministry is Spirit-empowered ministry.

The pattern of ministry in the New Testament church was to ensure that every believer was empowered by the Spirit and taught how to minister and witness using spiritual gifts. If the church today is to be the church Jesus Christ intends it to be, we must follow the same New Testament pattern. Every pastor and church leader must make leading believers into the baptism in the Holy Spirit a primary goal in ministry. They must not stop there, however. They must go on to teach their people how to minister in the Spirit's power through the manifestation of spiritual gifts. They should teach them by both word and example.

The first step in preparing believers to minister in the power of the Spirit is to help them receive the Holy Spirit. Consequently, every pastor and spiritual leader should regularly lead his or her church in times of asking for the Spirit. Leading the people in prayer to be filled with the Spirit should be a regular exercise in Pentecostal churches. Pastors and leaders should do this both when the church gathers for corporate worship and when they go about their daily ministries.

My sincere prayer is that you will make leading people into Spirit-anointed ministry a priority as you fulfill your calling. The fulfillment of God's mission around the world depends on it.

Chapter 11 ~ Ministry in the Spirit

Questions for Discussion and Reflection

1. How would you respond to the idea that the gifts of the Holy Spirit ceased after the death of the apostles and the completion of the New Testament?

2. What should a pastor do if there is a lack in the manifestation of spiritual gifts among the members of his church?

3. How can church leaders guard against spiritual gifts being used in extreme ways that harm the church, like what was happening in Corinth?

4. How would you apply the principles concerning praying with believers to receive the Holy Spirit in your ministry?

Chapter 11 ~ Ministry in the Spirit

BIBLIOGRAPHY

Arrington, French L. 1994. *Christian Doctrine: A Pentecostal Perspective*. Vol. 3. Cleveland, TN: Pathway Press.

———. "Luke." 1999. In *Life in the Spirit New Testament Commentary*, edited by French L. Arrington and Roger Stronstad. Grand Rapids, MI: Zondervan.

Flattery, George M. 2009. *A Biblical Theology of the Holy Spirit: Old Testament*. Springfield, MO: Global University.

Gee, Donald. 1980. *Concerning Spiritual Gifts*. Rev. ed. Gospel Publishing House. Kindle edition.

Harris, Ralph W. 1973. *Spoken by the Spirit: Documented Accounts of "Other Tongues" from Arabic to Zulu*. Springfield, MO: Gospel Publishing House.

Hesselgrave, David J. 1993. "A Missionary Hermeneutic: Understanding Scripture in the Light of World Mission." *International Journal of Frontier Missions* 10, no. 1 (January 1): 17–20.

Hodges, Melvin L. 1977. *A Theology of the Church and Its Mission: A Pentecostal Perspective*. Springfield, MO: Gospel Publishing House.

Holdcroft, L. Thomas. 1999. *The Holy Spirit: A Pentecostal Interpretation*, Revised. Abbotsford, Canada: CeeTec Publishing.

Horton, Stanley M. 2001. *Acts: A Logion Press Commentary*. Rev. ed. Springfield, MO: Gospel Publishing House.

———. 2005. *What the Bible Says About the Holy Spirit*. Rev. ed. Springfield, MO: Gospel Publishing House.

Miller, Denzil R. 2005. *Empowered for Global Mission: A Missionary Look at the Book of Acts*. Springfield, MO: Life Publishers International.

———. 2008. *In Step with the Spirit*. Springfield, MO: AIA Publications.

———. 2009. *Power Encounter: Ministering in the Power and Anointing of the Holy Spirit*. Revised. Springfield, MO: AIA Publications.

———. 2014. *Missionary Tongues Revisited: More Than an Evidence: Recapturing Luke's Missional Perspective on Speaking in Tongues*. Springfield, MO: PneumaLife Publications.

———. 2017. *Acts: The Spirit of God in Mission*. Africa's Hope Discovery Series. Springfield, MO: Africa's Hope.

Palma, Anthony D. 2001. *The Holy Spirit: A Pentecostal Perspective*. Springfield, MO: Logion Press.

Stronstad, Roger. 1984. *The Charismatic Theology of St. Luke*. Peabody, MA: Hendrickson.

———. 2003. *The Prophethood of All Believers: A Study in Luke's Charismatic Theology*. New York: Sheffield Academic Press.

York, John V. 2000. *Missions in the Age of the Spirit*. Springfield, MO: Logion Press.

AIA Publications
580A Central Street
Springfield, MO, USA

www.ingramcontent.com/pod-product-compliance
Lightning Source LLC
Chambersburg PA
CBHW061636040426
42446CB00010B/1445